Fertility Differences in a Modernizing Country

A SURVEY OF LEBANESE COUPLES

Fertility Differences in a Modernizing Country

A SURVEY OF LEBANESE COUPLES

by David Yaukey

PRINCETON UNIVERSITY PRESS
PRINCETON, NEW JERSEY
1961

FOREWORD

The Near East shares with other newly industrializing regions the seeds of very rapid population growth. Like the Far East and Latin America, many of the largely Moslem countries of the Eastern Mediterranean region can rather readily employ modern medicine and public health to reduce death rates, and can expect traditional values and customs to sustain a high birth rate. Thus these countries face rates of population growth of 2.5 to 3.5 per cent and heavy burdens of child dependency.

We can infer these facts from scattered observations in the Near Eastern countries themselves, and from data gathered in countries with roughly analogous economic and social circumstances. Only in Egypt (and Turkey, if it is considered as part of the Near East) is there a useful series of population censuses. Substantial national data on births and deaths are even more scarce. There is almost no published information on differences in fertility within Near Eastern countries, or as to whether deliberate control of family size is practiced by numerically important segments of the population.

In this book Dr. Yaukey shows that women in isolated Lebanese villages have very large families, whether the women are Christian or Moslem. In other words, he shows that the fertility of rural Lebanon is what would be expected in a pre-industrial agrarian area. In Beirut, on the other hand, both religion and education are shown to be strongly

v

associated with fertility. The number of children borne by educated urban Christian women is no more than about half the number borne by rural women. The careful description and analysis of these fertility differentials in this book provide a good beginning toward the eventual understanding of a crucial problem: how are the fertility changes essential to orderly economic and social progress in this region to take place?

This book is based on a field survey conducted in Lebanon under Dr. Yaukey's supervision when he was on the faculty of the American University of Beirut. He analyzed his data and wrote his manuscript while a Research Associate at the Office of Population Research. His colleagues at the Office congratulate him on the collection of valuable data under difficult circumstances, and for his careful analysis.

Ansley J. Coale, Director
Office of Population Research
Princeton University

PREFACE

This book reports the fertility differences found among 900 women interviewed in Lebanon. The idea for such a survey came out of a discussion with Dr. Hanna Rizk at the American University at Cairo in the summer of 1957. Dr. Rizk then was finishing the field work for a similar survey of Egyptian women. He not only encouraged a parallel effort in Lebanon, but also supplied his field materials as a starting point.

This book is the result of continuous financial, moral, and intellectual support over the more than three years since that summer. The field phase, directed from the American University of Beirut, extended from the early spring of 1958 to midsummer of 1959. The analysis and reporting phase, performed at the Office of Population Research, Princeton University, took from the fall of 1959 to this writing, in the spring of 1961.

Funds for the field phase came from the School of Arts and Sciences of the American University of Beirut, where the author was teaching, and from the Social Research Center of the American University at Cairo, where Dr. Rizk was affiliated. The main support during the field phase, however, and all of the support during the analysis and reporting phase came from The Population Council, Inc. The generosity of these organizations created an enviable situation for a researcher.

Nevertheless, financial support alone would not have made the study possible. The subject of the study was a sensitive one.

The director of the study was an outsider. To help in gaining local cooperation, several physicians and representatives of medical and welfare organizations in Lebanon were willing to commit themselves as sponsors of the study. The physicians were Dr.'s Adma Abu-Chdid, Musa K. Ghantus, Saniyya Haboub, Mustafa Khalidy, Joseph J. McDonald, Ibrahim H. Mufarig, Abdullah Rifai, Gabriel Rifka, and Susan Williamson. Other individuals expressed the support of their organizations; Dr. Gabriel Rifka for the Social Health Center in Ras Beirut, Dr. Howard Mitchell for the School of Public Health of the American University of Beirut, Dr. Frederic Tabah for the regional office of the United Nations, Mrs. Habiba Yekan for the Women's Moslem Association, Eunice Baber, R. N., for the School of Nursing of the American University of Beirut, Mrs. Fuad Najjar for the Village Welfare Society, and Dr. Mustafa Khalidy for the National School of Nursing. Interviewers went into the field with signed requests for cooperation from all of these sponsors. They also had identification cards and written legitimation from Mr. Nadim Harfouche, Director General of the Ministry of Social Affairs for the Republic of Lebanon. It is difficult to imagine how the research could have been performed without the willing cooperation of all of these respected Lebanese and friends of Lebanon.

Several people offered their specialized talents in criticizing the field plans, in helping to train the interviewers, and in many small ways throughout the field phase. Among these were Dr.'s Charles Churchill, Frederic Tabah, Saniyya Haboub, Susan Williamson, Lincoln Armstrong, Salem Khamia, Mr. Joseph Gholl, and Miss Isobel Pifer.

Nevertheless, the burden of responsibility fell on a loyal and resourceful staff. Mrs. Marion C. Hope not only served as consultant and helped to train the interviewers, but also performed the difficult role of liason between the project staff and the community. The unilingual project director leading research in another language necessarily leans very heavily on his multilingual research assistants. Three graduate students in the Department of Sociology and Anthropology of the American University of Beirut performed this unusually demanding role with skill and dedication; they were Mr.'s Latif Abul-Husn, Habib Habib, and Nabil Dajani. Mrs. Grace Azrak Hajjar, my colleague in that department, was invaluable in locating qualified interviewers and in helping to train them. To the administration of the university go my thanks for their willingness to remove administrative obstacles when they appeared.

Being an interviewer for this particular study required a high level of skill; remaining an interviewer required a high level of courage, loyalty, and faith. I hope that listing their names will be partial repayment to these ladies for the personal investments they made in the study: Siham Abu-Haidar, Siham Adham, Evelyn Haddad, Sophie Riahi, Hannah Shaheen, Naheel Da'dis, Aida Dinletir, Maliha Fakhoury, Leila Ghandour, Asma Hishmeh, Afifi Jabir, Nameeda Kanawaty, Nora Katbeh, Wadad Khuri, Margaret Schweiri, and Lydia Tannous.

The Office of Population Research at Princeton University proved the ideal location for making the most of the data. It is impossible to list all of those at the Office who have given their time, efforts, criticisms, and sympathy throughout the past year and a half. From the beginning, Robert G. Potter, Jr., has acted as my interested and encouraging guide. He, Philip C. Sagi, Ansley J. Coale, and Charles F. Westoff gave incisive criticisms upon request and share the credit for any tightness which the analysis possesses. The author alone is responsible for any limitations in the product.

David W. Yaukey

May, 1961

TABLE OF CONTENTS

APPENDICES

LIST OF TABLES IN TEXT

LIST OF TABLES IN APPENDICES

FERTILITY DIFFERENCES IN A MODERNIZING COUNTRY:

A SURVEY OF LEBANESE COUPLES

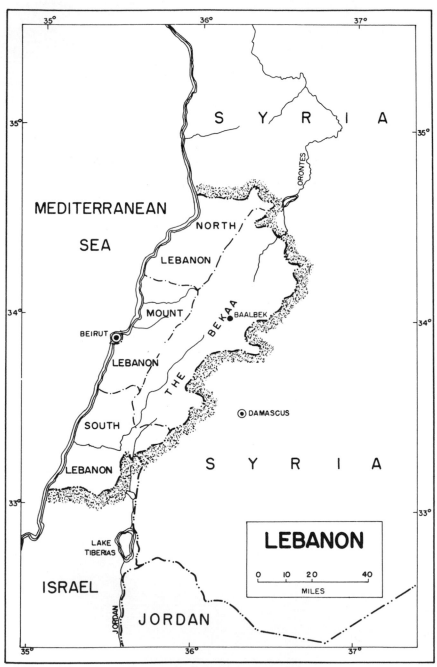

MEDITERRANEAN
SEA

SYRIA

ORONTES

NORTH
LEBANON

MOUNT

BEIRUT

LEBANON

THE BEKAA

BAALBEK

⊙ DAMASCUS

SOUTH

SYRIA

LEBANON

LAKE
TIBERIAS

ISRAEL

JORDAN

JORDAN

LEBANON

0 10 20   40
MILES

Office of Population Research, Princeton University

CHAPTER I

THE SETTING

A. <u>Introduction</u>

It is conventional to start books on fertility of underdeveloped countries dramatically. One cites the density of the existing population, the fall of the death rate, the persistence of the high birth rate, then points to the imminent population explosion. This is appropriate for studies of India, Egypt, and the many other recognized population trouble spots in the world.

It may be less appropriate for Lebanon. Imminent overpopulation is not universally accepted as an overriding problem for Lebanon. Nor is there a conspicuous birth control movement or program. A Lebanese is likely to think of overpopulation first as the problem of neighboring Egypt.

The main reason, perhaps, is that Lebanon views itself as already started in its modernization, rather than struggling to get started. From his recent social survey of the Near East, Daniel Lerner supports this view.[1] "Lebanon . . . scores well ahead of all Arab neighbors on every index of modernity. Lebanon has the highest proportion of people who live in cities; earn and spend cash; attend school and are literate; read newspapers; see films and hear radios."

The present book focuses on the fertility differences that have accompanied Lebanon's modernization.[2]

---

1. Daniel Lerner, The Passing of Traditional Society: Modernizing in the Middle East (Glencoe, Ill.: The Free Press, 1958) p. 169.

2. There has been a series of studies on another small modernizing country, Puerto Rico. Of the books resulting, the one most comparable with the present book is Paul K. Hatt, Backgrounds of Human Fertility in Puerto Rico: A Sociological Survey (Princeton: Princeton University Press, 1952). Later, more intensive studies are reported in two later books: J. Mayone Stycos, Family and Fertility in Puerto Rico: A Study of the Lower Income Group (New York: Columbia University Press, 1955) and Reuben Hill, J. Mayone Stycos, and Kurt W. Back, The Family and Population Control: A Puerto Rican Experiment in Social Change (Chapel Hill: University of North Carolina Press, 1959).

1

B. The Population of Lebanon

Lebanon lies at the eastern tip of the Mediterranean. Geographically it is the smallest of Near Eastern countries, about half the area of Israel to its south and about 6 per cent of the area of Syria to its north and east. Within Lebanon's borders live about one and one-half million people. Their density is approximately 325 persons per square mile, higher than any other Near Eastern country, including Israel.[3]

The density of population decreases as one moves eastward from the cities on its Mediterranean coast, up the Lebanon mountain range, across the high Bekaa valley, and on to the Anti-Lebanon mountain range at its eastern border. It is the most urbanized of Near Eastern countries. About 400,000 people, more than one-fourth of the population, live in the metropolitan area of its largest city, Beirut.

Lebanon is distinguished from its neighbors by its religious heterogeneity. The latest official figures concerning religious composition are based on a count taken in 1943. According to those figures, Christians slightly outnumbered Moslems. The Moslems were split between the Sunni and Shiite sects. Most of the Christians were Catholics, but a large minority belonged to various Orthodox sects.

---

3. The most recent published attempt to describe Lebanese population was made by Kingsley Davis, and is reported as a chapter of Human Relations Area Files, Inc., The Republic of Lebanon, Volume I (New Haven, Conn.: Box 2054 Yale Station, 1956) pp.   This chapter, plus some unpublished sources, served as the basis for our necessarily general description of Lebanese population.

It is generally agreed that the last trustworthy census of Lebanon was taken in 1932. Statements about more recent times usually are estimated from 1932 figures, with rough additions and subtractions based on reported vital statistics. Davis casts doubt upon the reported vital statistics as well.

C. Religion in Lebanon

   1. Introduction

         Lorimer has pointed out that the history of religious followers

as a social group (sect) may affect that religion's position on fertility and

its readiness for social change.[4] It seems plausible that the history of

relations among religious sects in any particular society might lead to

particular religious attitudes toward fertility and toward change.

         If this is true of any country it would be true of Lebanon.

"Through the ages the Lebanon, thanks to its valleys and hills, has provided places of refuge for individuals with unpopular beliefs and for
groups representing minorities.   Christian anchorites, Moslem Sufis,
Druze ascetics preferred its caves and recesses to the pleasures of the
world.   Numberless are the grottoes dedicated to the Virgin and other
saints.   Maronite sectarians in the seventh century, fleeing Jacobite
persecution in North Syria, find in North Lebanon a haven of peace.
Druze devotees, considered heretic by the orthodox Moslems, enter in
the eleventh century from the south.   Dissident Shiites, escaping Sunnite fury, infiltrate at different times from different places.   More
recently Armenians and so-called Assyrians, remnants of communities
subjected to Ottoman persecution, make their way into it.   All are provided therein with an opportunity to live their own lives in their own
ways.   The minority of the plain may thrive in the mountain to become
a majority, the heterodoxy to an orthodoxy.   Maronites, Druzes, and
Shiites develop into nationalities or quasi-nationalities — and so they
remain."[5]

   2. History of the Major Sects [6]

         Nominally the largest single sect in Lebanon is the Maronite

Christian. This is an indigenous sect which took refuge in the Lebanese

mountains in the seventh century. In the fifteenth century it accepted

the discipline of the Vatican, while maintaining limited autonomy.   For

---

4. Frank Lorimer, Culture and Human Fertility (Paris: UNESCO, 1954)
    pp. 183-198.

5. Philip K. Hitti, Lebanon in History (London: MacMillan & Co., Ltd.,
    1957) p. 8.

6.. The main source for the statements below is the Human Relations Area
    Files handbook, The Republic of Lebanon, Volume I, op. cit. Particularly
    relevant are pages 37-40 by Philip K. Hitti and pages 97-112 by Raphael
    Patai.

most of its history it has been treated as a separate community or nation under the millet system of Arab and Turkish rulers. Maronite contact with France has been long and close. French Jesuits took an early interest in the sect, setting up schools for its members as early as the seventeenth century. The French government applied pressure on the Ottoman rulers for their protection, and even sent troops briefly for their protection after the massacre of Maronites in 1860. More recently, Maronites have established close ties with the United States through heavy emigration. It can be viewed as a particularly western-oriented, well-educated, and prosperous group.

The Greek Orthodox, descended from the Byzantine church, is the second largest Christian sect in Lebanon. It is rather loosely organized on a national or regional basis; the head of the Lebanese Greek Orthodox community is the Patriarch of Antioch, who resides in Damascus. Historically, its main outside affiliation has been with the Russian Orthodox Church and many of its priests are Russian educated. It is generally considered more Middle Eastern in orientation than the Maronites. The Orthodox in Beirut are numerous, and are considered a prosperous and secular group.

The Moslems are associated with the conquering wave which spread through the Near East and beyond, beginning in the seventh century, a wave which left the Christian dissidents isolated in the Lebanese mountains. Unlike the Christians, they have not been identified with European supporters, but rather with the prevailing Moslem administration and majority group in the Near East. Their nostalgia for the past flowering of Islam is sometimes cited as a reason for their supposed relative conservatism today. The two main sects of Moslems, Sunnis and Shiites, are well represented in the present Lebanese population.

Lebanon contains many smaller sects, each with its own peculiar history, outlook, and identity as a separate community. But most of the women interviewed for the study reported here belonged to one or another of the major sects.

Each of these sects can be viewed as a social group as well as a class of believers in a particular faith. Each has its own history of relations with other sects and with the outside. This has implications for the present as well as the past.

3. Continued Importance of Religion

Among the countries of the Near East, Lebanon probably could be singled out as the most secular in outlook. At the same time it is a plural society, the organization of which is largely based on the integration of (rather than the assimilation of) its many religious groups.

This religious pluralism expresses itself in many aspects of its social organization. Members of a particular sect tend to settle in particular regions of the country if they are farmers, and in particular quarters of the city if they are urban. They still tend to take up particular occupations, although these occupational predilections appear to be diminishing. They tend to go to their own parochial schools. Every Lebanese must identify himself with some religious group officially; having no religious identity in Lebanon would be as inconceivable as having no racial identity in the United States.

5

This pluralism is expressed in the method of distributing political power. Lebanon became a Republic in 1943. The constitution included Article 95.

". . . Article 95 laid it down that, at least provisionally, the (religious) communities should be equitably represented in public offices and in the Ministry, in so far as that did not detract from the welfare of the State.

". . . the President of the Republic was always a Christian, and with the exception of the first president a Maronite. To counterbalance this, the Prime Minister was normally a Sunni Moslem, and the other Ministries were distributed among the different (religious) communities as equitably as possible. The Chamber of Deputies was so constituted as to represent the communities roughly in proportion to their numerical strength; every district elected a number of deputies belonging to the different communities living in it, but every deputy was elected not only by his co-religionists but by the whole electorate of the district. The maintenance of the balance between the communities was an important and often the most important consideration in the making of appointments in central and local administration alike."[7]

The last accepted census of Lebanon took place in 1932. One of the reasons for abstaining from further counts must now be clear. The present balance of power in Lebanon is based on the assumed continuance of the slight Christian majority found in the 1932 census. To find that the religious composition of the population has changed would be to rock the political boat. This illustrates the continuing importance of religious identity in Lebanon.

4. Religious Positions on Fertility and Fertility Control

The religious teachings reaching Lebanese couples would be those transmitted and interpreted by their local religious leaders. The people to ask about religious positions on fertility in Lebanon, therefore, would be the Lebanese religious leaders.

---

7. A. H. Hourani, Syria and Lebanon: A Political Essay. (New York: Oxford University Press, 1946), p. 182.

Unfortunately, our information on this subject is scanty. The author did send some of his students at the American University of Beirut to find from their various religious leaders their positions on fertility and fertility control. But only a few leaders were interviewed, and the students' reports should be considered impressionistic.

The position of the Maronite sect on fertility and fertility limitation is exactly that of the Roman Catholic church. This position needs no repetition here beyond the reminder that it is against mechanical and chemical methods of control, permissive of the rhythm method, and generally considered pro-natalist in effect.

The position of the Greek Orthodox leaders on fertility was less specific. Generally, they took the view that one should have as many children as God will give him. Generally, they viewed any form of voluntary fertility control as wrong. But it is possible that, with a less clearly stated position than the Catholic one, Greek Orthodox leaders might be more flexible in their advice in specific cases.

There seems no appreciable difference between the Sunni and Shiite Moslem leaders in their attitude toward fertility and fertility control. High fertility is advocated as a commitment to the growth of the religious group and the spread of the true faith. Further, the limiting of fertility (or even the thought of limiting fertility) is an expression of lack of faith in the omnipotence of Allah to provide for all of his followers. The stand of the Koran on methods of fertility control is not specific and, unlike the Catholic position, is subject to various interpretations. It is clear, however, that two themes make the general Moslem position pronatalist in effect; numerical expansionism and fatalism.[8]

---

8. For a more complete discussion of the influence of the Moslem religion on fertility see Lorimer, op. cit, pp. 186-187.

On the basis of this very limited information, we would be unwarranted in stating that any of the religions is more pro-natalist than the others. All of them seem considerably more pro-natalist in effect than contemporary western Protestantism.

D. The Changing Lebanese Family

1. Introduction

Generalization about contemporary Lebanese society is dangerous. Published descriptions are fragmentary and often misleading. They consist mainly of standard historical works, anthropological studies of particular villages, recorded impressions of area residents or experts, and a very few limited social surveys.[9]

Most available sources have been used by Rafael Patai for his interpretive summary chapter on The Family in the Human Relations Files handbook on Lebanon.[10] Unless otherwise specified, the source for the generalizations made below are Patai's summary.

2. The Traditional Family

One is safer in describing the family ideal as it is defined in Lebanese traditions than in describing the increasing deviations from this ideal. Let us start by listing those many features that are common to the traditions of all religious sects.

The family is extended, patrilineal, patrilocal, and patriarchal. The traditional household consists of a senior couple, their married sons, the wives and children of those sons, and perhaps some widowed or divorced

---

9. Probably the most extensive social survey effort was Charles W. Churchill, The City of Beirut (Beirut, Lebanon: Dar El-Kitab, 1954).

10. Human Relations Area Files, op. cit.

8

sisters of the men.   Important kinship relationships are traced exclusively through the males.   At marriage, the wife goes to live with the husband and his family.   The senior male holds the dominant authority in the household.

Women are not veiled and secluded to the extent specified by the traditions of more conservative Moslem countries.   But there is a definite division of labor along sex lines and a limitation of social contacts to members of one's own sex.

The extended family and the male lineages connecting them are very important in the social structure.   The extended family acts as a unit of economic production, social control over its members, and welfare for its members.   One's kinship relations determine one's loyalties, social status, and political power.   Success or failure is attributed to families as well as to individuals.

This traditional family system supports high fertility in many ways.   Marriage is almost universal, and girls are married very early, sometimes as early as twelve years of age.   There is little place in the community for a mature man or woman without sons.

The strength and power of the family as a unit is measured in terms of the number of sons born into it.   The father gauges his success as head of the family largely in terms of the number of children — and especially sons — he has produced.   These children are supposed to supply him prestige, economic wealth, power against his enemies, and comfort in his old age.   A woman gauges her success, as well, by the number of children (sons) she has produced.   Furthermore, the earlier she produces sons the sooner she can achieve the relatively powerful and leisurely position of mother-in-law in an extended family household. A childless woman is viewed with mixed contempt and commiseration, and is subject to the possibility of her husband (if he is a Moslem) taking a second wife or divorcing her.

The family system described so far could be considered traditional in all major Lebanese religious sects. However, matters of marriage are handled by the religious authorities of each sect, not by civil authorities. And there are some differences in the religious laws involved.

For Moslems, marriage is a contractual relationship officiated by the Moslem court. A bride price (mahr) is agreed upon by the two families involved. Part of this is paid immediately by the father of the groom to the father of the bride for the latter to use in supplying the bride with personal wealth and clothing for the wedding. Another part of the bride price is deferred, to be paid to the bride in the case of divorce. Although this practice is not written into Maronite Catholic nor Greek Orthodox marriage law, it is not clear to what degree it has been accepted informally.

Divorce is easiest for Moslems, more difficult for Orthodox Christians, and disallowed for Catholics (including Maronites). The act of divorce for Moslems involves a statement of intent by the husband in front of qualified witnesses; nor is there a stigma attached to it. It is discouraged however, by the strain it places on the relations between families, by the cost of the deferred portion of the bride price which the divorcing husband must pay, and by the cost to the husband's family of any future wedding. Divorce is considered an extreme step, the main justification for which is the failure of the woman to produce sons. Remarriage of both husband and wife is usual after the divorce. There is no reliable evidence on the actual

10

frequency of divorce and remarriage among Moslem families in Lebanon.

Moslem permissiveness of polygyny up to four wives is widely known. However, as Lorimer points out, the incidence of polygyny in present-day stable Moslem societies is probably far less than in the days of Moslem expansion.[11] Its incidence, even among traditional Lebanese Moslem families, is unknown. Even in conservative segments of the Moslem population, probably well below ten per cent of the married males have more than one wife. When polygyny does occur, the reason is probably the failure of the first wife to produce sons.

3. Western Impact on the Traditional Family

The direct competitor to this traditional family model has been the modern western urban family model. It is not an extended family but a nuclear one, with emphasis on the father, the mother, and their children as the most important unit. It is not patrilocal but neolocal, with the new couple setting up separate residence largely independent of where the husband's father lives. It is not strictly patrilineal in that it recognizes relationships through the mother as well. It is not patriarchal to nearly the extent of the traditional Lebanese family, and tends to accept the ideal of equality and cooperation and companionship between the sexes in family relationships. It forbids polygyny and at least discourages divorce.

---

11. Lorimer, op. cit., p. 186.

The family system in a culture tends to be consistent with the rest of the culture. To the degree that other aspects of western culture are accepted in Lebanon, the traditional family in Lebanon might be challenged. Feminism or sexual egalitarianism is inconsistent with the male dominance of the patriarchal traditional family. Western technology challenges the extended family as a production unit by reorganizing production and taking the worker away from the home. The emphasis on secular education creates a need which the traditional family cannot supply by itself. Urbanization that accompanies western technology creates a new social environment to which the extended family unit is ill adapted.

The impact of western ideas might be more evident if we look at one aspect of the traditional family which has direct relevance to marital fertility; the age of women at marriage. In the traditional system, the woman is married at a very early age, often as early as twelve years. Under the western system the potential husband no longer has the economic security of his father's extended family to offer, but must defer his marriage until he has established his independent economic position, perhaps involving some delay for education. His partner is not selected by his family but by himself. He seeks someone able to play the role of companion and equal, a woman who has spent some time in obtaining secular education and experience approximating his. The woman is no longer in such a hurry to marry and have sons, since achieving the mother-in-law role no longer implies the dominance and leisure that it did in the extended family. The unmarried state for the woman, especially in her teens, is no longer an anomoly; it can be viewed as a period of personal growth and/or preparation for newly available independent possibilities of employment. This picture is purposely exaggerated. However, it can hardly be denied that western influences discourage very early marriage of women.

12

But is it _realistic_ to speak of the western urban family system and the rest of western culture as having a strong impact on Lebanon? Patai states flatly that ". . . in Lebanon the process of modernization or westernization of the family is more advanced than in neighboring Jordan and Syria."[12] Several explanations are possible. Geographically, Lebanon is located like a buffer zone between the West and much of the Moslem world. Its commercial emphasis has permitted a high degree of urbanization. The small size of the country and the high development of communication media have made possible the rapid dissemination of new ideas. The Christian elements in the population have furnished an avenue for European ideas. Heavy emigration to (and some re-immigration from) the United States in particular has created numerous agents of westernization, even in the villages. There is every reason that western impact on Lebanon should be relatively great.

It is unlikely, however, that the western impact on the traditional family has been the same for all segments of the population. The history of modern social changes in other societies leads us to expect a _pattern_ of spread for new ideas. One would expect the changes to be accepted in the cities before the villages. In the cities, one would expect the changes to be accepted earlier by the better-educated persons and those whose occupations put them in closest and most frequent contact with western culture. Moreover, one would expect the changes to occur more readily in those groups which have had the longest and closest affiliation with the source of the new ideas; thus one would expect the Christians to be more ready to accept the ideas of the West.

These are plausible suppositions. We will see later how well they fit with observations on differential fertility in Lebanon.

---

12.   _Ibid._, p. 254.

E. Origin of the Study

The situation described for Lebanon is true, in varying degrees, of her Near Eastern neighbors. For instance, the traditional family model described for Lebanon would also do for the traditional family model in Egypt, in general. In Egypt, as well, the main external challenge to the traditional pattern is from the West. It is true that Egypt is more homogeneously Moslem, and that the spread of western patterns there is judged to be less wide than in Lebanon. But it is probably safe to say that the point of origin and the direction of change are roughly the same in the two countries.

These, at least, were the thoughts which came to the author when he was talking with Professor Hanna Rizk at the American University at Cairo in the summer of 1957. Professor Rizk was in the midst of his field work for a fertility survey in Egypt, interviewing a large sample of urban, semi-urban, and village women, Christian and Moslem. His purpose was to describe and explain differential fertility in Egypt. The idea of making a comparable survey in Lebanon came out of that meeting. From that time, Professor Rizk has been generous in enabling the author to use the Egyptian survey as a model in designing the Lebanese survey.[13]

By the following spring of 1958, we had obtained the financial support required. The main sponsor has been, and is, The Population Council. Additional support for the field work came from the American University of Beirut, where the author was teaching, and from the Social Research Center of the American University at Cairo, with which Professor Rizk is affiliated.

---

13. The results of the Egyptian survey are recorded in Hanna Rizk's dissertation presented to the Faculty of Princeton University in Candidacy for the Degree of Doctor of Philosophy in June 1959, titled Fertility Patterns in Selected Areas in Egypt.

Preparation for the interviewing took most of the next year. It was not until the spring and summer of 1959 that the final interviewing took place.   Since that time, the author has been analyzing and reporting the results at the Office of Population Research, Princeton University, through the continuing generosity of The Population Council.

CHAPTER II

THE METHOD

A. Design of the Study

The goals of the study were two: (1) to determine to what degree marital fertility in Lebanon differed on the basis of social background characteristics of couples; and (2) to find by what means these differences in fertility were brought about.

In settling on these goals, we eliminated several others: The study was not descriptive but explanatory in intent; the goal was not to describe the fertility of Lebanon as a whole, but rather to point out the interrelationships between fertility and other characteristics for a cross section of Lebanese women. The study was not oriented toward any action program, but was a preliminary inquiry on a rather general level. The study paid no attention to fertility outside of marriage.[1] Finally, no attempt was made to measure fertility in particular time intervals, such as in annual birth rates; rather the subject was the total fertility of particular women.

To achieve the goals of the study, three classes of information were gathered about each married woman or couple; (1) the social background characteristics of the partners before marriage and of the couple immediately after marriage, (2) the history of that marital behavior which could have directly affected the woman's fertility, and (3) the fertility history of the woman. Attitudes relevant to fertility and fertility control were solicited as supplementary information.

Interviews with about 900 Lebanese married women were the source of all data.

---

1. Lebanese norms are quite strict about fertility outside of marriage, and marriage is almost universal.

B. Contents of the Interview Schedule [2]

1. Social Background Characteristics

The social background characteristics included religion, type of community of residence, education, occupation, and rooms per capita.

Since the population to be interviewed was not limited to any particular marriage cohort, it was necessary to decide upon some standard and meaningful time referent for all social background characteristics.[3] The times chosen were (1) the last five years before marriage, for the premarital characteristics of the future partners and (2) the first five years after marriage, for the postmarital characteristics of the couples. For instance, there were questions to determine the type of community of residence of the woman before marriage, of the man before marriage, and of the couple immediately after marriage.[4]

---

2. This chapter confines itself to the choice of contents for the interview schedule. It further confines itself to that content relevant to the following results chapters. The full content of the interview schedule is recorded in Appendix E: Interview Schedule and Interviewer Instructions. The basis for eliminating some data from further analysis is recorded in Appendix C: Evaluation of the Data. Also see Appendix B, Technical Note 3: Unusual Formal Features of the Interview Schedule.

3. Measuring the characteristics as of the time of interview would have caused two difficulties in interpretation: (1) The time of interview could have occurred early in some marriages and late in others, confusing the comparison of characteristics that change with marriage duration (e.g., rooms per capita), (2) To the degree that the interview followed part of the fertile period, one would have little guidance in guessing whether the social background characteristic was more likely to be the cause or the effect of fertility. Since social background characteristics were to be treated as possible causes in this study, their time referents were chosen to be (1) standard in relation to the date of marriage and (2) previous in time to most of the fertile period.

4. The use of such an early time referent is not without difficulties. Most important, it requires the respondent to remember a time period which may have preceded the interview by several decades. Interpretability may be bought at the cost of precision.

2. Immediate Determinants of Fertility

Some western demographers are becoming aware of unwarranted assumptions with which they are likely to be burdened in explaining differences in international fertility. Norman Ryder, for instance, expresses concern over this shortcoming:

" . . . (the) assumption is . . . commonly made that differences in fertility between populations are solely the consequence of differences in fertility regulation. This may be true on balance, but it is clearly false in detail. Progress in fertility research will be considerably enhanced by . . . the accumulation of reproductive life histories, perhaps in diary form, of menstruation, copulation, conception, fetal death, and birth. This will facilitate a more satisfactory evaluation of the extent to which differing cultural patterns contribute to overt fertility differentials independently of fertility regulation." [5]

The most systematic specification of possible immediate determinants of fertility differences is an article by Kingsley Davis and Judith Blake.[6] We followed their scheme in specifying the possible immediate determinants of fertility for the present study.

Davis and Blake categorize immediate determinants into four main classes.[7] The variables included in our interview schedule are listed below within the classes to which they apply.

---

5. Norman B. Ryder, Chapter 18, "Fertility," in Philip M. Hauser and Otis Dudley Duncan (eds.), The Study of Population (Chicago: University of Chicago Press, 1959), p. 418.

6. Kingsley Davis and Judith Blake, "Social Structure and Fertility: An Analytical Framework," Economic Development and Cultural Change, April 1956, Vol. 4, No. 3, pp. 211-235. The immediate determinants of fertility were called "intermediate variables through which any social factors influencing the level of fertility must operate." Page 211.

7. Ibid. p. 212.

I.   Factors Affecting Exposure to Intercourse

    A.   Those governing the formation and dissolution
        of unions in the reproductive period

        Woman's years of age at marriage
        Man's years of age at marriage

    B.   Those governing the exposure to intercourse
        within unions

        Periods of separation from the husband
        Periods of abstinence from intercourse
        Frequency of intercourse during the first
        year after marriage
        Frequency of intercourse between first live
        birth and next conception

II. Factors Affecting Exposure to Conception

        Periods of lactation
        Use of contraceptive methods

III. Factors Affecting Gestation and Successful Parturition

        Stillbirths
        Spontaneous abortions
        Induced abortions

We cannot claim perfect coverage of all of the classes mentioned by Davis and Blake. By concentrating on marital fertility, we eliminated from consideration those factors in class IA referring to non-marriage, broken marriage, or sexual unions other than marriage. Among those classes of factors we did attempt to cover, we had least precision on the subject of fecundity. Aside from these limitations, however, the interview schedule sought information on most of the factors mentioned by Davis and Blake.

3. Fertility

The procedure for obtaining fertility information was simple in design, if not so simple in practice. The whole marital history of the woman was reviewed. The number of months after marriage when each pregnancy ended was recorded. The fate of the pregnancy was recorded as well. The result was a history of live births specifying their time of occurrence.[8]

4. Attitudes

Our main interest was in opinions on ideal family size. Each woman was asked what family size and composition she would advise for another woman like herself. If she gave specific advice she was further asked to describe the ways in which she thought her husband would agree or disagree with this advice.[9]

During its year of preparation, the interview schedule was pre-tested and revised extensively. The final schedule was in simple Arabic. It was administered to about 900 Lebanese married women, who composed "the sample."

C. The Sample

1. Limits of the Population

Certain types of women were eliminated from the population at the outset. Women who were not Lebanese Nationals probably comprised less than 10 per cent of the women resident in Lebanon, usually had lived

---

8. This history also furnished the information on stillbirths, spontaneous abortions, and induced abortions, listed under "immediate determinants" above.

9. We also included questions referring to rationalizations for use or non-use of contraception. These data were relatively unreliable and unrelated to the main goals of the present analysis.

Several other questions were asked, not to supply substantive information, but to allow the control of extraneous factors. See "control variables" in Appendix E: Interview Schedule and Instructions.

20

in Lebanon for short periods of time, and — since many were refugees —
might have been unusually suspicious and uncooperative. Women who
were married for less than five years had too little chance to accumulate
fertility histories. Women married more than once might have had quite
different patterns of social background and fertility with each husband, and
thus would have been very difficult to analyze. For this variety of reasons,
the population was confined to women who were Lebanese nationals, married
only once, and married for more than five years.

2. Sampling Design

The goals of the study were to determine and to explain the relationship between social background factors and fertility. A prime necessity,
then, was to interview women who varied greatly with respect to the three
main social background factors: religion, socioeconomic status, and rural-
urban residence. Furthermore, we wished to be able to talk about the
fertility correlates of each of these background factors separately, controlling the effects of the other factors. Therefore, it was necessary to
find women representing all combinations of the background factors. The
combinations of characteristics sought are presented below:

Residence	Socioeconomic Status	
	Low	High
Urban	1	2
Rural	3	4

The goal was to represent all major religions in cells 1, 2, and 3. We did
not actively seek women for cell 4, since we believed that class to be
relatively small in Lebanon.

We purposively selected a number of small areas expected to
include women of the desired types. In each of these areas, we attempted
to interview all eligible women. The resulting sample is not a probability

21

sample of the Lebanese national population, nor of any other population.[10]
The field procedures for actually selecting the cases are described below.

D. Gathering the Data

1. Sponsorship

Although the government had no direct stake in the study, the Ministry of Social Affairs did give its permission for the interviewing to take place. Indeed, it was cooperative enough to furnish each interviewer with an identification card, complete with photograph, legitimizing the interviewer's activities.

Government sponsorship, of course, was not enough and even had negative value in some factions. Fortunately, two highly respected professional groups, doctors and social workers, gave their support. Thus every interviewer went armed with a pack of thirteen signed sponsorship cards to show at her discretion in opening the interview.[11]

---

10. Had we sought a probability sample of the national population, political considerations would have frustrated us. The Lebanese insurrection of 1958 ended only a few months before interviewing was to start. Random choice of sampling units from the national population probably would have selected many units dangerous to interview. The necessary substitution of units probably would have cast doubt upon the representativeness of the sample.

   The decision for full enumeration, rather than sampling, within purposively selected areas was an economic one. The question was whether, within a given budget, we could represent more people by random sampling within selected areas or by full enumeration of a smaller selection of areas. The field costs seemed to depend more on the number of areas than on the number of interviews. Since no detailed maps or lists existed, each area had to be mapped, at least, in order either to draw a sample or assure full enumeration. Local rapport had to be gained in each area by careful preparation and, in some cases, by lengthy visits. We judged that random sampling within chosen areas was not justified on the basis of economy.

11. See Appendix B, Part 2: Gaining Rapport.

In the villages this rather formal sponsorship was supplemented by informal trust. We spent hours visiting the village headman, explaining the importance of the study — as best we could — and setting the environment for maximum cooperation and accuracy of response.

2. Interviewers

All of the interviewers were Lebanese women. During the year of preparation before the final field work most of the final 14 interviewers had gone through three training periods and one pretest experience.[12]

3. Choosing Respondents

In choosing Beirut respondents, the goal was to represent all major religious sects and, within each sect, to get as wide a range of socioeconomic status as possible. To supply respondents with these characteristics, four of the forty-odd administrative districts in Beirut were selected, mapped, and divided into blocks. Each interviewer was assigned one block at a time, with specific orders to proceed from a given starting point and in a given direction. The necessity for full enumeration was stressed, and interviewers were instructed to call back repeatedly.

Two neighboring, extremely isolated villages were chosen. They were alike in all major observable respects save that one was populated by Maronite Catholics and the other by Sunni and Shiite Moslems. All qualified women in each of these villages were sought for interview. Village interviewing was done on a quick-assault basis, to outdistance the spread of rumors in such cohesive communities.[13]

---

12. See Appendix B, Part 1: Research Staff.

13. See Appendix A, Part 3: Social Backgrounds of the Sample.

4. The Product

The result of the field work was 909 interviews, 613 of them from Beirut and 296 from the two villages; the overrepresentation of the city was dictated by the sample design. If one defines as a "refusal" any stated refusal, cut-off interview, or known avoided interview, then the rates were 12 per cent in Beirut, 15 per cent in the Moslem village, and 8.5 per cent in the Christian village. We have no reason for thinking that the women who refused were different in any important way from the women interviewed.[14]

14. See Appendix A, Part 2: Attrition and Bias.

CHAPTER III

DESCRIPTION OF FERTILITY DIFFERENCES

A. Introduction

   1. Content of the Chapter

      The remainder of this book will describe and analyze the differences in fertility experienced by women of different residence, socio-economic status, and religion. The present chapter has the task of simple description.[1]

   2. Division of the Sample

      The women interviewed could have become married at any time from the turn of the century to the summer of 1954. Some of them long since had completed their fertile periods; others had been married as little as five years. The women, then, can be thought of as falling into two generations of about a quarter of a century each.

      What we will call the older generation of women consists of all women who were first married in 1928 or before and whose first marriage lasted at least thirty years.[2] These 139 women, we assume, all had exhausted their fecundity, or capacity to reproduce.

      What we will call the younger generation includes all 693 women who first married between 1929 and 1954. The vast majority of them were still married and probably fecund at the time of the interview.[3]

---

1. For more complete information on the distributions of social background characteristics in the sample see Appendix A, Part B: Social Backgrounds of the Sample.

2. Women married in or before 1928 but whose first marriages had ended less than thirty years later were eliminated from the analysis reported in this chapter.

3. Included in the younger generation are 47 women who had been widowed or divorced or separated before the interview but at least five years after the beginning of the marriage.

      A total of 11 women who would have fallen into either generation were eliminated because their responses were demonstrably very inconsistent. See Appendix A, Part A: Attrition and Bias.

3. Measures of Total Fertility

Since all women in the older generation are presumed to have completed their fertile periods, their fertility is easily described. The fertility of any woman is the number of children she has born alive. For any class of women, the fertility is summarized as the mean live births per woman in that class.

This measure, however, is not usable for the younger generation. Classes of younger generation women could vary in the years married per woman represented. What is needed is a single statistic which can summarize the fertility experience of a class of women of incomplete fertility, which will control class differences in the average years of exposure, and which will be analogous in meaning to the mean live births per woman for the women of complete fertility.

The total fertility rate is such a measure. We computed a total fertility rate for each class of women in the younger generation by summing the period-of-marriage specific rates for that class.[4]

---

4. The total fertility rate usually summarizes the specific fertility rates of age-of-woman classes. However, there seems no reason for not applying the same principle to period-of-marriage specific rates. See Ryder, op. cit., pp. 405-406.

The steps for obtaining this measure for any class were as follows: (1) Five successive five-year periods were measured off from the date of marriage. (Preliminary investigation had shown almost no live births after twenty-five years of marriage.) (2) The number of women completing each period of marriage was recorded. (3) For each period, the total live births occurring in that period to women who completed that period was recorded. (4) The total live births in a period to women completing that period was divided by the total number of women completing that period. (5) The mean live births per woman for all periods of marriage were summed to obtain the total of the means or the total fertility rate.

These steps are illustrated in Appendix F, Table F-1.

The total fertility rate resulting can be viewed as a synthesis of experience of cohorts married in the various intervals over a twenty-five year span.   It also can be viewed as a projection of the completed fertility of classes recently married.   As a projection, it minimizes the effect of fertility trends already under way and, of course, takes no account of trends that might occur in the next twenty years.   Its main advantages are its summarizing function and comparability with the mean live births per woman of completed fertility.[5]

4. Comparisons with an Egyptian Survey

The Lebanese survey was modeled after a recent study conducted in Egypt under the direction of Hanna Rizk.   The Egyptian sample included (a) 2,334 urban women who were a random sample of Cairo and the Muharram Bay District of Alexandria and (b) 3,057 rural women obtained by a complete enumeration of three villages.   Whenever possible in this chapter, we will present not only results from the Lebanese survey, but also the most comparable results from the Egyptian survey.[6]

---

5. Summary figures for whole "generations" might be misleading if fertility had been changing radically by marriage cohort within the generations.   There seems to have been little variation in mean live births per woman by decade of marriage for the older generation as a whole; see Appendix F, Table F-2. With respect to total younger generation, year-of-marriage classes did not vary appreciably in mean live births by period of marriage; see Appendix F, Table F-3.

6. At this writing, the results of the Egyptian survey have not been published.   They are recorded in Hanna Rizk's dissertation, op. cit.

B. Differences Among Religious Sects

The interviewers asked the postmarital religious sect affiliation both for the woman and for her husband. These two questions proved redundant. Endogamy within religious sect was almost complete. Only 3 of the 139 older generation women married across sect lines; 1 of them across Christian-Moslem lines. Only 18 of the 693 younger generation women married across the sect lines; 7 of them across Christian-Moslem lines.[7] With very few exceptions, then, the religious sect of the husband can be taken as that of the wife as well.

Were there fertility differences among the Moslem sects and among the Christian sects, or can one talk meaningfully about Moslems as a whole and Christians as a whole? Table III-1 presents the total fertility of each sect, both in the older generation and in the younger generation, classified by residence immediately after marriage.

There appear to be no significant fertility differences (1) among Sunnis, Shiites, and Druze or (2) among Maronites, other Catholics, and Orthodox Christians.[8] This holds for either generation and for either type of residence. The number of cases involved does not permit the conclusion that no differences would be found in a larger sample. Nevertheless, one seems justified in talking about two classes of religion in the rest of the analysis: (1) Moslems (Sunni, Shiite, Druze) and (2) Christians (Maronite, other Catholic, Orthodox). The homogeneity within these two classes seems great enough to avoid being misled.

---

7. In these statements Druze are treated as a Moslem sect.
8. We will attempt to warn the reader of differences in fertility which we believe probably due to chance. The basis for such warnings will be rather arbitrary interpretations of standard tests of significance of difference.

TABLE III-1

TOTAL FERTILITY BY RELIGIOUS SECT OF HUSBAND AND RESIDENCE OF COUPLE AFTER MARRIAGE

Residence and religious sect	Older generation		Younger generation	
	Number of women	Mean live births per woman	Number of women*	Total fertility rate
City				
Moslem sect				
Sunni	34	7.26	160-17	6.45
Shiite	1	**	33-2	6.83
Druze	2	**	9-1	6.17
Christian sect				
Maronite	14	4.86	71-8	3.63
Catholic, not Maronite	4	4.75	58-10	3.81
Orthodox	13	4.46	82-15	3.65
Town or Village				
Moslem sect				
Sunni	12	6.67	66-7	7.45
Shiite	22	8.09	116-6	7.65
Druze	1	**	1-0	**
Christian sect				
Maronite and other Catholic	27	6.56	86-17	7.56
Orthodox	5	7.80	10-2	4.08
Total	135***		692****	

* In this and all future tables reporting total fertility rates, the n of each class of women is represented by two figures, separated by a hyphen. The figure to the left of the hyphen is the number of women in the class having completed the first five year period of marriage and serving as the basis for that period-of-marriage specific fertility rate. The figure to the right of the hyphen is the number of women completing the fifth five year period of marriage and serving as the basis for that period-of-marriage specific fertility rate. The n's for the second, third, and fourth periods of marriage are not presented in the table. The two figures reported represent the range of n's for specific rates included in the total fertility rate.

** Inadequate number of women to furnish meaningful average.

*** Eliminated three cases in which husband and wife did not belong to the same religious sect, one case in which both claimed no religious identification.

****Eliminated one case where both claimed no religious identification.

C. Differences by Rural-Urban Residence

     A series of questions in the interview schedule allowed us to establish the residence of the couple or partners at three points in time, (1) during the last five years before marriage,(2) during the first five years after marriage, and (3) at the time of the interview. In all classifications, city refers to a community of more than 20,000 with more than half the labor force nonfarmers at the time of residence; all other communities are classed town or village. Most important was the community of residence immediatel after marriage.

     The hypothesis was that couples who had lived in cities immediatel after marriage were likely to have had lower fertility than couples who had lived in towns or villages immediately after marriage, regardless of religion. Table III-2 presents the relevant data.. Total fertility by place of residence is recorded for each generation and each religion.

     The patterns of differences are almost identical for the two generations. This leads one to suspect that whatever rural-urban fertility differences exist are of rather long duration, probably antedating recent industrialization.[9]

     Fertility of noncity women was quite high, irrespective of generation or religion; it ranged from 6.75 to 7.65 live births per woman. In one of Rizk's Egyptian villages with split religion, he found the completed fertility of Moslems to be 7.61 and of Christians to be 7.44.[10] Various surveys of rural sections of Indian provinces report completed fertility ranging from 5.8 to 6.6 children ever born.[11] Rural fertility in Lebanon, then, seems about

---

9. Comparisons between the absolute size of figures from one generation to another is not warranted. First, smaller differences between figures in the older generation might have been caused by less precision in older women's responses about their social characteristics. Second, figures for the younger generation omit experience between the 25th and 30th years of marriage. Only the pattern of differences is comparable.

10. Op. cit., Table V-7, page 106.

11. Ansley J. Coale and Edgar M. Hoover, Population Growth and Economic Development in Low-Income Countries: A Case Study of India's Prospects (Princeton: Princeton University Press, 1958) pp. 47-48.

TABLE III-2

TOTAL FERTILITY BY RESIDENCE OF COUPLE AFTER MARRIAGE AND
RELIGIOUS CLASS OF HUSBAND

Religion and residence	Older generation		Younger generation	
	Number of women	Mean live births per woman	Number of women	Total fertility rate
Moslem				
Town or village	35	7.49	183-13	7.65
City	38	7.21	202-20	6.53
Christian				
Town or village	32	6.75	96-19	7.18
City	32	4.69	211-33	3.70
Total	137*		692**	

* One woman was eliminated because she and her husband claimed no
religious identification. Another woman was eliminated because she
was Moslem and her husband was Christian. These remaining 137
cases will be included in all future tabulations by major religion in
this chapter.

** One woman was eliminated because she and her husband claimed no
religious identification. The remaining 692 cases will be included
in all future tabulations by major religion in this chapter.

as high as that in two countries frequently used as examples of high fertility.
In neither the Lebanese nor the Egyptian survey were differences between
noncity Moslems and noncity Christians found to be significant.

Urban fertility in Lebanon, on the other hand, depended on religion.
Among the Moslems, the difference between city and noncity fertility was
small in both generations, so small that it could be attributed to chance. In
sharp contrast, Christian city women in the older generation had fertility
about 69 per cent as high as noncity women. Christian city women in the
younger generation had fertility about 52 per cent as high as noncity women.

Rizk reports the same pattern of differences, in lesser magnitude, for Egypt. His figures for completed families are roughly equivalent to our figures for the older generation. Whereas Moslems interviewed in cities had 7.07 live births, Christians (mostly Copts) had 5.54 live births.[12]

In both surveys, then, small or nonexistent rural-urban differences were indicated among Moslems, but large ones were indicated among Christians.

Since we had asked more than one question about residence, we were in a position to probe into the timing of residential influences in greater detail. Unfortunately, any conclusions drawn from this analysis must remain highly tentative due to the very few cases which had mixed residential histories. Among the Christians, any span of urban residence, whether during the five years before marriage or the five years after marriage, was associated with considerably lower fertility.[13] Christian couples who moved from villages to cities some time during their fertile period had total fertility somewhere between village nonmigrants and city nonmigrants, apparently depending on the point in the marriage when they moved.[14] All this suggests that, for the Christians, any urban residence was related to markedly different fertility, no matter when in the lifetime that residence may have occurred. (Urban influences on Moslem fertility were negligible.)

---

12. Rizk, Op. cit. Derived from Table III-14b, page 48.

13. See Appendix F, Table F-4.

14. See Appendix F, Table F-5.

D. Differences by Socioeconomic Status

1. Introduction

Our hypothesis was that couples of higher socioeconomic background would have lower fertility. The hypothesis held that this would hold among both Christians and Moslems, among both city residents and noncity residents.

Our — admittedly crude — measures of socioeconomic status are (1) the highest level of education achieved by either member of the couple and (2) the rooms per capita in the dwelling unit the couple inhabited most of the first five years after marriage. In the case of the noncity couples, we also know (3) whether the husband had, as his main occupation during the first five years after marriage, farming or some nonfarming occupation.[15]

In describing the socioeconomic differentials, we choose to emphasize the results for the younger generation over those for the older generation. The results for the older generation seem considerably less stable and reliable.[16]

2. Differences in the Towns and Villages

Table III-3 presents the total fertility rates by education of couple, rooms per capita after marriage, and farming vs. nonfarming occupation for younger generation couples who lived in towns or villages during the first five years after marriage.

---

15. More detailed responses on occupations were found relatively unreliable. See Appendix C: Evaluation of the Data.

16. Figures summarizing the fertility of older-generation classes are usually based on very few cases. Furthermore, the reports on education, housing conditions, and occupation by the older women are more suspect. See Appendix C: Evaluation of the Data.

   Tabulations for the older generation, parallel to those for the younger generation in this portion of the text, are recorded in Appendix F, and will be referred to by footnote.

TABLE III-3

TOTAL FERTILITY RATES FOR YOUNGER GENERATION TOWN OR
VILLAGE RESIDENTS, BY SOCIOECONOMIC STATUS AND
RELIGION OF HUSBAND

	Moslem		Christian	
Socioeconomic status	Number of women	Total fertility rate	Number of women	Total fertility rate
Education of couple				
Both illiterate*	103-6	7.64	29-6	8.61
Either literate	80-7	7.61	67-13	6.61
Rooms per capita after marriage**				
0.6 or less	133-9	7.69	45-8	7.99
0.7 or more	50-4	7.45	51-11	6.60
Occupation of husband after marriage***				
Farmer	132-8	7.73	58-12	7.90
Nonfarmer	48-5	7.53	36-7	5.79

*   "Illiterate" means unable to read and write more than own name,
according to the claim of the respondent.

**   Obtained by dividing rooms available by 1 for person over 20 years
old, by 2/3 for person between 10 and 20, by 1/3 for person less
than 10.

*** Eliminated three Moslems and two Christians whose husbands were
non-self-supporting most of the first five years after marriage.

      The fertility of Moslem couples did not differ by education, rooms
per capita, nor occupation. However, there seems to have been a slight
inverse relationship between socioeconomic status and fertility among the
Christian couples. This difference reaches a size where it can hardly be
attributed to chance in the case of occupation, Christian nonfarmers having
only 5.79 live births compared with 7.90 for Christian farmers. The same
pattern of results, but with smaller differences, was found for couples of the
older generation.[17]

17. See Table F-6.

These differences among Christians might be misleading unless investigated further. Included in the population in Table III-3 are couples who later migrated to cities. Table III-4 describes the fertility of women who were not only living in a town or village after marriage, but also were interviewed in a village.

TABLE III-4

TOTAL FERTILITY RATES OF YOUNGER GENERATION INTERVIEWED
IN VILLAGES, BY SOCIOECONOMIC STATUS AND
RELIGION OF HUSBAND

	Moslem		Christian	
Socioeconomic status	Number of women	Total fertility rate	Number of women	Total fertility rate
Education of couple				
Both illiterate	101-6	7.62	29-6	8.61
Either literate	68-5	7.80	41.7	8.11
Rooms per capita after marriage				
0.6 or less	130-8	7.70	42-8	7.87
0.7 or more	39-3	7.74	28-5	9.04
Occupation of husband after marriage*				
Farmer	131-8	7.72	57-11	7.93
Nonfarmer	36-3	7.71	12-2	11.21

* Eliminated two Moslems and one Christian whose husbands were non-self-supporting immediately after marriage.

Apparently migration later in the marriage depleted the town and village higher-status classes considerably. Those few high-status couples who did stay seem to have been at least as fertile as the low-status non-migrants. The table for the older generation women does not contradict this conclusion. [18]

18. See Table F-7.

Rizk came to the same conclusion from his comparisons among women interviewed in three Egyptian villages. "In summary, the rural data in the sample reveal distinctly the absence of any significant differences in fertility by education, occupation, or religion."[19]

It is difficult to sort out the urban influences from the socio-economic influences in interpreting these results. One can choose at least two alternate lines of reasoning. (1) Better educated, better housed, more skilled villagers are those who move; when they do move (if they are Christians) they are influenced by city living to have fewer children. (2) Villagers who move to a city are a select group, having those values both making cities attractive to them and (if they are Christians) making large families un-attractive to them; Christians would have had smaller families even had they remained in villages.

3. Differences in the Cities

Table III-5 presents the fertility by education and rooms per capita of younger generation women who were living in cities during the first five years after marriage. (It should then be noted that obtaining an elementary education certificate in Lebanon involves a minimum of five years of formal schooling.)[20]

The expected inverse relationship between socioeconomic status and fertility does appear to have occurred among Moslems. The better educated and better housed Moslems had approximately one and one-half fewer children than did their opposite numbers. Although a similar pattern of differences appears among Christians, the differences were considerably

---

19. Rizk, Op. cit., p. 107.

20. Table F-8 shows the minimum years of formal schooling required for the various educational classes used in this study.

TABLE III-5

TOTAL FERTILITY RATES OF YOUNGER GENERATION RESIDENT IN CITY AFTER MARRIAGE, BY SOCIOECONOMIC STATUS AND RELIGION OF HUSBAND

Socioeconomic status	Moslem		Christian	
	Number of women	Total fertility rate	Number of women	Total fertility rate
Elementary education certificate				
Neither possesses	116-10	7.05	80-17	3.96
Either possesses	86-10	5.85	131-16	3.47
Rooms per capita after marriage				
Less than one	57-7	7.08	28-4	4.51
One to two	89-9	6.83	95-18	3.65
Two or more	56-4	5.44	88-11	3.43

smaller and could be attributed to chance. The equivalent tabulation for older generation women allows no conclusion of differences by socioeconomic status.[21]

Rizk made similar tabulations for his Egyptian survey. "In order to assign a socioeconomic status to the wives under study, information about occupation of husband, household conditions, and education of husbands was utilized in formulating a socioeconomic index." All wives are classified into three classes on the basis of this index, Class I having the highest socioeconomic status.[22]

---

21. See Table F-9.

22. Ibid., page 21.

Rizk concludes from his tabulation of (older generation) women of completed fertility that "the fertility of both (religious) groups is inversely associated with class, except for the Moslems among Class III, where the rate is slightly lower than that for Class II.[23] His findings for the (younger generation) incomplete families were generally the same.[24]

Here, for the first time, one meets a discrepancy between Rizk's findings in Egypt and our findings in Lebanon. Both studies agree in finding socioeconomic differences among younger generation city Moslems. But Egyptian Christians showed the same differentials of at least the same magnitude while Lebanese Christians showed very small or nonexistent differentials by socioeconomic status. Finally, Rizk found such differentials to have existed in both generations while we can find such evidence only in the younger generation.

E. Relationships among Socioeconomic, Residential, and Religious Influences on Fertility

1. Introduction

Earlier in this chapter we came to certain conclusions about rural-urban and religious differentials in fertility. We noted that among Christians, though not among Moslems, city couples had far lower fertility than town or village couples. We also noted that city Christians had considerably lower fertility than did city Moslems. The reader at that point may have wondered whether these differentials might not be explained by the higher socioeconomic status of city Christians as compared with either non-city Christians or city Moslems.

---

23. Ibid., page 47.

24. Ibid., pp. 67-70.

Two specific questions need answers: First, did city Christians have lower fertility than noncity Christians in the same socioeconomic classes? Second, did city Christians have lower fertility than city Moslems in the same socioeconomic classes?

2. Socioeconomic Status and Rural-Urban Differences

Table III-6 presents differences between city and noncity fertility within socioeconomic and religious classes. The figures in the table refer to the degree to which noncity fertility was in excess of city fertility for that class of women. To the degree that socioeconomic status explained rural-urban differences, one would find the figure for each socioeconomic class to be smaller than the figure for the total unclassified population at the bottom of the table.

The rural-urban differences among Moslems previously have been shown to be small and questionable. These differences seem to shrink even further within socioeconomic classes. This would throw into even greater doubt the effect of urban residence on Moslem fertility.

The situation appears quite different for the Christians. The rural-urban fertility differences do not seem to be consistently smaller within socioeconomic classes than for the unclassified total population. Only in the best-educated and best-housed classes do the rural-urban differences appear appreciably smaller than for the total population. The immediate reason for this seems to be the considerably lower fertility, by rural standards, of highest-class town-or-village women. Noncity couples with two or more rooms per capita had a rate of 4.78; noncity couples having an elementary certificate had a rate of 5.42. We have reason to believe that a high proportion of these few women later migrated to cities.[25] Therefore,

---

25. See pp.   above.

this observation would not seem to negate the general conclusion: For Christians, rural-urban differences in fertility were not appreciably explained by socioeconomic differences.

Although one cannot use the data for the older generation as a basis for conclusions, it should be mentioned that nothing in these data seem to refute the above conclusions.[26]

TABLE III-6

EXCESS TOTAL FERTILITY RATES OF TOWN OR VILLAGE RESIDENTS OVER CITY RESIDENTS IN YOUNGER GENERATION, BY SOCIOECONOMIC STATUS OF COUPLE AND RELIGION OF HUSBAND*

Socioeconomic status	Moslem	Christian
Education of couple		
Both illiterate	0.29	4.40
Either literate but no elementary certificate	0.62	3.09
Either with elementary certificate	**	1.95
Rooms per capita after marriage		
Less than one room	0.72	2.70
One to two rooms	**	4.10
Two or more rooms	**	1.35
Total population	1.12	3.48

* Based on Tables F-10 and F-11.

** No figure available for town or village women in class.

Rizk presents partially comparable results for women of completed fertility in Egypt. He classified both his urban sample and his villagers according to education of husband. His illiterate (unschooled) class would represent the same degree of education in either village or city. The vast majority of the villagers were illiterate. The appropriate question is: Were the city vs. village differences greater in the total

---

26. See tables F-12 and F-13.

40

population than in the illiterate class alone?

Apparently they were not. For the Moslems, the city vs. village difference for the total was 0.54 live births; for the illiterates alone it was 0.43 live births. For the Christians, the city vs. noncity difference for the total was 1.90 live births; for the illiterates alone it was 2.05 live births.[27]

Thus in neither Egypt nor Lebanon was there evidence that socioeconomic status differences explained rural-urban differences among Christians.

3. Socioeconomic Status and Religious Differences in the City

Our second question was: Did city Christians have lower fertility than city Moslems in the same socioeconomic classes? Table III-7 presents the differences between the Christian and Moslem fertility within socioeconomic classes for those women resident in a city during the first five years after marriage. To the degree that socioeconomic status explained religious differences, one would find figures for each socioeconomic class to be smaller than the figure for the total unclassified population, at the bottom of the table.

TABLE III-7

EXCESS TOTAL FERTILITY RATES OF MOSLEMS OVER CHRISTIANS IN YOUNGER GENERATION RESIDENT IN CITY AFTER MARRIAGE BY SOCIOECONOMIC STATUS*

Elementary education certificate		Rooms per capita after marriage	
Neither member possesses	3.09	Less than one	2.57
Either member possesses	2.38	One to two	3.18
		Two or more	2.01

Total population 2.83

*Based on Tables F-14 and F-15

---

27. Rizk did not himself make the comparisons reported here. We obtained the data for making the comparisons from his Tables V-7 and III-14b. Only the split-religion village (Shameya) was used, in order to make possible comparisons within religion.

41

Apparently socioeconomic differences give little help in explaining religious differences in fertility in the city. Religious fertility differences within socioeconomic classes were not appreciably smaller than in the unclassified population. Moreover, uneducated Christians had a considerably lower total fertility rate (3.96) than did elementary-educated Moslems (5.85).[28] Christians living in less than one room per capita after marriage had a lower fertility rate (4.51) than did Moslems living in two or more rooms per capita (5.44).[29]

Similar tabulations for the older generation show nothing to contradict a conclusion that religious fertility differences in the city have had little relation to socioeconomic differences.[30]

Analogous results are available for (older generation) women of completed fertility in Rizk's samples of Cairo and part of Alexandria. It seems that the religious fertility differences within socioeconomic classes were, on the average, slightly smaller than the differences for the total population. The weighted mean of the within-class differences was 1.02; the difference for the total population was 1.53. However, socioeconomic differences far from completely explained fertility differences between religions. The differences did not disappear within socioeconomic classes. Moreover, Class III Christians were less fertile than Class II Moslems (6.56 vs. 7.36 live births); Class II Christians were less fertile than Class I Moslems (5.41 vs. 6.00 live births).[31] Considerable religious differences seem to remain unexplained by socioeconomic differences in Cairo and Alexandria as well as in Beirut.

28. See Table F-14 .
29. See Table F-15.
30. See Tables F-16 and F-17.
31. Ibid., Table III-14c.

F. Summary

The pattern of fertility differences seems remarkably stable and general. With very few exceptions, the same patterns seem to have applied both to women in the older generation and women in the younger generation. Moreover, very few differences were found between the pattern in Lebanon and the pattern in Egypt.

The influences of urban residence and of high socioeconomic status on fertility have operated rather independently. The results in general lead to the conclusion that patterns of fertility differentials associated with rural-urban residence and socioeconomic status were different for the two major religious classes. The exception to this was in the villages, where no fertility differences by socioeconomic status were found in either religious group. By eliminating from attention the marginal class of high socioeconomic status villagers, one can schematically summarize the fertility of six main social types in the younger generation.[32]

	Moslem	Christian
Rural uneducated	high	high
Urban uneducated	high	low
Urban educated	moderate	low

The main fertility differential was a rural-urban one among Christians; this differential among Moslems was negligible. A secondary differential was a socioeconomic one among city Moslems; this differential was much smaller among city Christians. Therefore, Christian fertility was much lower than Moslem fertility in the city, particularly among the uneducated.

---

32. "High" is taken to mean a total fertility rate above 7. "Moderate" is taken to mean a total fertility rate between 5 and 7. "Low" is taken to mean a total fertility rate below 5.

CHAPTER IV

INTRODUCTION TO THE ANALYSIS OF FERTILITY DIFFERENCES

A. Social Background Types

1. Defining the Types

The vast majority of couples in our sample fell into six homogeneous types defined on the basis of residential background, education, and religion. Of the 801 couples married in or after 1920, 648 were included in the social background types:[1]

    a. Uneducated village Moslem couples, neither member of which had an elementary educational certificate; 184 women.

    b. Uneducated village Christian couples, neither member of which had an elementary educational certificate; 76 women.

    c. Uneducated city Moslem couples, neither member of which had an elementary educational certificate; 136 women.

    d. Uneducated city Christian couples, neither member of which had an elementary educational certificate; 96 women.

    e. Educated city Moslem couples, either member of which had a Lebanese Brivet or some higher educational degree; 49 women.[2]

    f. Educated city Christian couples, either member of which had a Lebanese Brivet or some higher educational degree; 107 women.

A total of 153 marginal cases were eliminated for one or more of the following reasons: They were (1) migrants, having lived in one type of community immediately after marriage but having been interviewed in another type of community, (2) village educated couples, either member of

---

1. Inclusion of the 97 couples married before 1920 in the social background types might have confused the analysis of behavioral differences among the types. Older women (those married earlier) were known to have answered many of the questions with less accuracy than younger women; see Appendix C: Evaluation of the Data. Within any type, changes in fertility behavior over a long span of time would make summary statements about that type less meaningful. These problems were decreased by limiting the types to women married between 1920 and 1954.

2. In Lebanon, an elementary educational certificate requires a minimum of five years of formal schooling; a Lebanese Brivet requires a minimum of nine years of formal schooling.

44

which had received an elementary educational certificate, (3) city couples

which had a _medium_ level of education, that is, the better-educated mem-

ber of which had received an elementary certificate but no higher degree,

(4) women whose husbands identified with a major religious class other

than their own, (5) couples claiming Jewish identification or no religious

identification.

2. Fertility of the Types

The total fertility rates of the six social background types are

presented in Table IV-1.   These rates display faithfully the pattern of

fertility differences pointed out for the younger generation in Chapter III.

Village fertility was high, and showed negligible religious differences.

Within the same education class, Christian fertility was markedly lower

in the city than in the villages; no such difference is seen among the Mos-

lems.   Within the city, moderate fertility differences based on education

were found among Moslems, but much smaller ones were found among

Christians.[3]

TABLE IV-1

TOTAL FERTILITY RATES OF SOCIAL BACKGROUND TYPES

Social background type	Number of women	Total fertility rate
Village, uneducated		
1. Moslem	184-28	7.43
2. Christian	76-19	8.16
City, uneducated		
3. Moslem	136-30	7.35
4. Christian	96-35	4.14
City, educated		
5. Moslem	49-5	5.56
6. Christian	107-16	3.44
Total	648	

3. Appendix Table F-18 presents the period-of-marriage specific fertility
   rates of the social background types. Appendix Tables F-19 through
   F-22 present the percentage distributions of each type with respect to
   religious sect, exact education of the couple, rooms per capita
   immediately after marriage, and decade of marriage.

B. Explaining the Fertility Differences

The purpose of Chapters V and VI will be to explain the differences in fertility among the social background types. They will do this by referring to our data on the immediate determinants of fertility behavior which could have affected the fertility of couples. The purpose will be to determine which behavioral differences among the social background types explain the fertility differences among the types.

These immediate determinants can be viewed as falling on a continuum between totally voluntary and totally involuntary. Voluntary determinants would include those methods used only by individual choice and with the goal of affecting fertility. Involuntary determinants would include all methods not involving individual choice by the marriage partners and/or not aimed at limiting fertility.

It is convenient to divide the immediate determinants we can study into two classes on this basis, although in some cases the assignments may seem arbitrary.[4] The involuntary determinants would be the fecundity of the couple, the age of the woman at marriage, prolonged separations from her husband, frequency of intercourse, and time spent nursing children. The voluntary determinants would include induced abortion and all appliance and non-appliance methods of conception control. When in doubt, we have labelled a method involuntary rather than voluntary. For instance, long periods of nursing might be used by some women to avoid conception, but the practice is also widely spread among other women not using it for this purpose; it is classed involuntary.

The analysis of involuntary determinants appears in Chapter V. The analysis of voluntary determinants follows in Chapter VI.

---

4. For a discussion of our choice of immediate determinants, see Chapter II, Part B, Section 1: Immediate Determinants of Fertility.

CHAPTER V

INVOLUNTARY DETERMINANTS OF FERTILITY

A. Introduction

Chapters V and VI will investigate the behavior of the couple during marriage for immediate causes of fertility differences among six social background types. In both of these chapters, it will be convenient to assume that the social background types do not differ appreciably in average fecundity, or capacity to bear living children.

Fecundity is the product of two factors: (1) the capacity to conceive and (2) the capacity to end pregnancy successfully. Preliminary investigation leads us to believe that the variation among the social background types on these two factors was small.[1] We will not be misled far by assuming that average fecundity was approximately the same for all six social background types.

This chapter investigates the other involuntary determinants of fertility; the age of the woman at marriage, frequency of intercourse, periods of separation, and periods of nursing.

Each of these determinants is taken up separately and treated as exhaustively as the data warrant. Three questions are posed: (1) How can this determinant have affected fertility? (2) Did the social background types differ with respect to this determinant? (3) To what degree does this behavior differential explain the observed fertility differences among the social background types?

Not all questions, of course, are approached for every determinant. In some cases we simply don't have the data. In other cases, one or more of the questions are clearly redundant.

_____

1. See Appendix D, Technical Note 2: Fecundity of Social Background Types.

B. Age of Woman at Marriage

    1. Nature of the Effect

        Common sense leads to a simple picture of the effect of a woman's age at marriage on her total marital fertility. A woman has a given number of years when she has the biological capacity to give birth (fecundity). If she spends all of those years in marriage (by marrying very early), then she will produce more children than if she spends only part of the period in marriage (by marrying later).

        We can see to what degree the experience of the Lebanese sample fits this picture. We can control the effect of determinants other than age at marriage by limiting our attention to women (married in or after 1920) who never attempted to control conception, never induced an abortion, and never were separated from their husbands for more than three consecutive non-pregnant months. In Table V-1 these women are classified by their reported ages at marriage.[2] For each age class, both the mean age at marriage and the total fertility rate of the women are presented.[3]

TABLE V-1

TOTAL FERTILITY RATES BY AGE OF WOMAN AT
MARRIAGE FOR WOMEN OF UNCONTROLLED
FERTILITY

Age of Woman at Marriage			Total Fertility	
Class limits	Number of women	Mean age	Number of women	Rate
11 to 13	28	12.5	28-8	7.28
14 to 17	163	15.5	163-34	7.74
18 to 22	136	19.7	136-33	5.65
23 to 27	44	25.1	44-11	4.46
Total	371		371	

2. We have classed reported age of woman at marriage in such a way that numbers ending in 5 fall near the midpoints of intervals. Preliminary evaluation of the data showed a tendency for women to report their ages in multiple of 5.

3. Sixteen eligible women were married at ages 28 or older. They are not included in this table because they were too few to furnish a stable total fertility rate.

48

Except for the youngest-married class, total fertility decreased systematically and markedly with increased age of woman at marriage. An increase in mean age of woman at marriage from 15.5 to 25.1 (9.6 years) was associated with a decrease in total fertility rate from 7.74 to 4.46 (3.28 live births). This would imply that, after about age 14, women of uncontrolled fertility and uninterrupted cohabitation lost about one live birth per three years of delay in marriage.[4]

Nevertheless, the total fertility rate of women married at ages 11 to 13 (7.28) was as low or lower than that of women married at ages 14 to 17 (7.74). The rate for the 11 to 13 age class should be viewed with caution since it is based on only 28 cases. However, similar results are reported by Lorimer for census populations of other countries.[5]

One possible explanation for the low fertility of very early marriers is suggested by Ryder:[6]

---

4. One might argue the following: (1) women of higher fecundity were more likely to have used birth control than women of low fecundity. (2) Women married at later ages were more likely to have used birth control than women married at earlier ages. (3) Therefore, the remaining (noncontrolling) members of older age-of-woman-at-marriage classes would have progressively lower average fecundity. If so, the elimination of birth controllers from the population would partially explain the apparent effect of age of woman at marriage on fertility.

   However, we performed a tabulation identical to the one reported in Table V-1 on a sub-population from which only 10 of 184 women had to be eliminated because of birth control; the social background type of uneducated village Moslems. The fertility differences associated with age-at-marriage differences for these women were as large as those reported in Table V-1 (See Table F-23). This leads us to conclude that selectivity by fecundity was not an important biasing factor in the results presented in Table V-1.

5. Lorimer, op. cit., pp. 30-32.

6. Ryder, op. cit., p. 418. Also see Sohan Singh and John B. Wyon, "An Epidemiological Study of the Population Problems in North India," Fifth International Conference on Planned Parenthood; Report of the Proceedings, 24-29 Oct. 1955, Tokyo, Japan. (London: International Planned Parenthood Federation.

49

"A high level of fertility in the early ages represents
an exposure to greater risk of damaging the reproductive
apparatus and thus may prejudice fecundity at later ages."

Our data do not permit us to explore this possibility for our Lebanese
sample.

Another possible explanation is that the years of exposure
added by very early marriage were subfecund years. There has been
considerable study of the onset of fecundity with aging of the woman.
Ryder concludes,[7]

"By weighing the information pooled from these sources
and making inferences about the behavior of statistical
aggregates, a model of fecundity may be constructed to
indicate variations of fecundity by age of woman. It is
probable that, for a birth cohort of women, aggregate
fecundity increases at first gradually and then rapidly
from the zero level in the early teens to a maximum
not far below unity in the early twenties . . ."

We do have indirect evidence that women aged 11 to 13 at
marriage in our Lebanese sample were relatively subfecund at the
time of marriage. The mean months between marriage and first live
birth for the 11 to 13 age class was 25.5. The mean months between
marriage and first live birth for women married at ages 14 to 17, 18
to 22, and 23 to 27 were 16.6, 15.6, and 16.6, respectively.[8]

Thus early subfecundity probably contributed to the relatively
low total fertility of women married at ages 11 to 13 in our sample.
After these ages, later marriage was associated with systematic and
marked reduction in total fertility among the women of uncontrolled
fertility.

_____

7. Ibid., pp. 417-18. Lorimer presents a model describing this process;
op. cit., p. 50. One of the pioneers in the study of "adolescent sterility"
has been M. F. Ashley Montagu, whose recent book on the subject is
The Reproductive Development of the Female (New York: The Julian
Press, 1957).

8. Only non-permanently-sterile women who had done nothing that might
have delayed their first birth were included in the population. The
results are recorded in Table F-24.

2. Differentials by Social Background Type

       Differential age of woman at marriage, then, <u>could</u> have had some effect on fertility differences. Whether or not it helps to explain the fertility differences among our social background types, however, depends on the answers to two questions: (1) Were there differences among social background types in the average age of women at marriage? (2) Were these differences related to differences in total fertility rates of the social background types?

TABLE V-2
MEAN AGE OF WOMEN AT MARRIAGE AND TOTAL
FERTILITY RATE BY SOCIAL BACKGROUND TYPE**

Social background type	Number of women	Mean years of age of woman at marriage	Total fertility rate
Village, uneducated			
1. Moslem	183*	17.2	7.43
2. Christian	76	18.1	8.16
City, uneducated			
3. Moslem	135*	17.9	7.35
4. Christian	96	21.2	4.14
City, educated			
5. Moslem	49	19.0	5.56
6. Christian	106*	21.1	3.44
TOTAL	645		

*One woman eliminated from this class because she did not know her age at marriage. This case was used, however, in computing the total fertility rate for the class.

**Table F-25 in the appendix presents the percentage frequency distributions of ages at marriage by social background type.

51

Table V-2 shows the mean age at marriage of the women in each social background type. The range of means is rather large, the four years between 17.2 to 21.2. Everything else being equal, Moslem women married earlier than Christian women, village women married earlier than city women, and (among the Moslems) uneducated women married earlier than educated women.

Table V-2 also presents the total fertility rates of the social background types. Although the rank correlation is not perfect, the major differences in mean age of women at marriage correspond to the major differences in total fertility rate.

3. As an Explanation of Fertility Differences

Differential age of women at marriage, then, could explain part of the fertility differences among social background types. But it is possible to estimate only very roughly and indirectly the degree of this effect. Table V-3 shows what we guess would have happened had all types of women had the same mean age at marriage, and had that mean been the one reported for the latest-marrying type, the uneducated city Christians.[7]

---

7. Corrected total fertility rates for the social background types were computed by the following formula:

$$T_c = T_u - \frac{F_x(A_L - A_x)}{5}$$

where T_c = the corrected total fertility rate for type x.

T_u = the uncorrected total fertility rate for type x.

F_x = the mean number of live births per woman in type x during the first five years of marriage.

A_L = the mean age at marriage of women in the latest marrying type.

A_x = the mean age at marriage of women in type x.

TABLE V-3

TOTAL FERTILITY RATES OF SOCIAL BACKGROUND TYPES
CORRECTED FOR DIFFERENCES IN MEAN AGE OF WOMEN
AT MARRIAGE

Social Background type	Total fertility rate		
	Uncorrected	Corrected*	Difference
Village, uneducated			
1. Moslem	7.43	5.94	1.49
2. Christian	8.16	6.81	1.35
City, uneducated			
3. Moslem	7.35	5.84	1.51
4. Christian	4.14	4.14	0.00
City, educated			
5. Moslem	5.56	4.68	0.88
6. Christian	3.44	3.41	0.03
Standard deviation	1.77	1.16	

The corrected rates should be interpreted with caution.[8]
They probably overestimate slightly the effect of age at marriage on
differential total fertility.[9]

Nevertheless, some conclusions do seem safe. Differential
age of women at marriage probably was a _major_ factor in causing fertility differences among the social background types. Correcting for
differential age at marriage appreciably decreases the dispersion in
fertility rates for the social background types. Moreover, differential
age at marriage helps to explain all of the _major_ fertility differences

8. The corrected rates involve three main assumptions: (1) If the women
   in early-marrying types had married later, they would not have changed
   their subsequent fertility-determining behavior to make up for later
   marriage. (2) The later fecundity of early-marrying women was not
   damaged by too-early fertility experience. (3) The distribution of women's
   ages around the mean would have remained the same even if the mean
   were changed.

9. This might have resulted from the use of only the first five-year period
   of marriage in correcting rates. The first five years of marriage usually
   result in higher fertility rates than later five-year periods, primarily
   because the first period includes fewer months of post partum sterility.
   The mean live births per woman during each five-year period of marriage
   are listed for each social background type in Table F-18.

between pairs of social background types; uneducated village Christians vs. uneducated city Christians, uneducated city Christians vs. uneducated city Moslems, uneducated city Moslems vs. educated city Moslems. However, most of the fertility variance among social background types remains unexplained by this factor alone.

C. Frequency of Intercourse

Our data on frequency of intercourse probably are relatively inaccurate. Our analysis of this factor deserves only a brief summary here.[10]

Very slight relationships were found between (1) reported coital frequency during the first year of marriage and (2) months between marriage and first conception. The relationships seemed linear in nature. The Pearsonian correlation coefficients for the two major age-of-woman-at-marriage classes were .06 and .09. Even these relationships may be spuriously large.

The coital frequency differences among the social background types were small: The median monthly coital frequencies for the types during the first year of marriage ranged from 17.9 to 24.5; for the period between the first live birth and the next conception the medians ranged from 11.7 to 18.6. Moreover, the pattern of coital frequency differences was not closely related to the pattern of fertility differences among the social background types.

We have no evidence that differential frequency of intercourse contributed appreciably to differential total fertility among the social background types.

---

10. A more complete description of the analysis is presented in Appendix D, Technical Note 3: Frequency of Intercourse as a Determinant of Fertility.

D. Prolonged Separations from Husband

By "prolonged separation" we mean separations lasting more than three consecutive months while the woman was not pregnant. Separations of this nature represented very small proportions of the total non-pregnant months for women of any social background type; the highest per cent was less than 2.[11] We can reject differential prolonged separation as an important determinant of fertility differences among our social background types.[12]

E. Prolonged Nursing of Children

1. Introduction

Some children are never nursed by their mothers; others are nursed until the mother becomes pregnant again. The normal period of nursing can vary not only from society to society, but also from class to class within the society.

Women may, of course, nurse their children for long periods for reasons of nutrition and sanitation. Mother's milk may have few competitors as a diet for a baby in an impoverished village. And — in the view of some public health nurses — sanitation is more easily achieved in nursing than in preparing other foods for the baby.

However, it is probable that some mothers use prolonged nursing as a method for delaying the conception of the next child. From his review of the literature, Ryder notes [13]

> "It is apparently a widespread belief that the mother who feeds her baby at the breast cannot become pregnant again until lactation ceases."

---

11. The population used in this tabulation does not include women married more than 25 years. The results are reported in Appendix F, Table F-26.

12. It should be noted, however, that the definition of social background types involved the elimination of postmarital migrant couples. Thus our types probably exclude couples most prone to separation.

13. Ryder, op. cit., p. 420.

One can pick up references to this belief from a wide variety of areas. For instance, Stix reports of the southern United States that " . . . the women who delayed the use of contraception depended to a great extent on prolonged nursing and associated amenorrhea to protect themselves against further pregnancy."[14] Singh and Wyon, studying villages in India, report, "There is a widely believed folk tale that women who are lactating cannot conceive . . ."[15] In our interviewing in Lebanon, prolonged nursing was frequently mentioned as one of the methods for delaying pregnancy known to the woman.

There would be justification, therefore, for treating prolonged nursing as a "voluntary" rather than an "involuntary" fertility determinant. We chose to call it involuntary because long nursing could have resulted from several considerations other than the desire to delay the succeeding pregnancy, unlike (for instance) contraception.

2. Nature of the Effect

The biological mechanism by which nursing might delay pregnancy is generally agreed upon. After a delivery a woman has a period during which she does not menstruate (postpartum amenorrhea), usually followed by one or more menstrual cycles during which no ovum is produced; during both of these periods she is infecundable. To quote Guttmacher,[16]

"Lactation's delaying effect on reimpregnation has a two-fold mechanism. First, it postpones the return of the menses; second, even when the menses return during lactation the first few menstrual cycles are frequently anovulatory."

---

14. Regine K. Stix, "Factors Underlying Individual and Group Differences in Uncontrolled Fertility," Milbank Memorial Fund Quarterly, (July 1940), p. 252

15. Sohan Singh and John B. Wyon, op. cit., p. 79.

16. A. F. Guttmacher, "Fertility of Man," Fertility and Sterility, vol. III (May-June 1952) p. 284.

Thus nursing could prolong the period of infecundability of the woman after delivery.

Some doctors believe that nursing does, on the average, detain the return of fecundability of women after birth. For instance, Sharman, from reviewing the studies on ovulation after pregnancy, concludes that "during the first nine months after parturition, the risk of conception is significantly lower among those who are breast-feeding their babies."[17] From her survey of southern United States rural and urban women, Stix concludes, "It is probable that the length of the postpartum period of amenorrhea depends to a great extent on the associated length of lactation."[18] Hyrenius found that early death of an infant was usually followed by proportionally shorter periods to next conceptions, and attributes this partly to the cessation of nursing caused by the death.[19]

Others caution that, while this effect of nursing might be true on the average, there is probably a wide variation among women in the degree to which this mechanism operates.[20] Still others are skeptical that it operates at all.

More research is required before we will know the exact limits of the effectiveness of this method of delaying pregnancy. We must proceed, however, with the limited understanding we have. Let us assume that continued nursing does, on the average, delay the reinstatement of fecundability in women for a few months. Would this help to explain the fertility differences among our Lebanese social background types?

17. A. Sharman, "Ovulation after Pregnancy," Fertility and Sterility, Vol. II (Sept.-Oct. 1951), p 386.
18. Stix, op. cit., p. 247.
19. H. Hyrenius, "Fertility and Reproduction in a Swedish Population Group without Family Limitation," Population Studies, 12, (Nov. 1958), p. 128.
20. Louis Henry, "Intervals between Confinements in the Absence of Birth Control," Eugenics Quarterly, 5(4) (December 1958), p. 204.

3. Differences among Social Background Types

In the context of describing the history of her pregnancies, each respondent was asked how many months, approximately, she had nursed each live born child. This supplies us with the data to approach two questions: (1) Did the normal nursing period vary appreciably from one social background type to another? (2) If it did vary, did it vary in such a way as to help explain the fertility differences among the social background types?

Table V-4 presents the mean months of nursing per child for each social background type.[21] The differences in average lengths of lactation are large, ranging from 18.9 to 7.0 months. Moslems nursed longer than Christians. Villagers nursed for longer than city residents. Mothers in uneducated city couples nursed for longer than mothers in educated city couples.

However, almost all of these differences are the opposite of those required to explain the fertility differences among the types. That is, the types having the longer average periods of nursing are those having higher — rather than lower — fertility.

Differential length of nursing could not help explain the major fertility differences among social background types. To the degree that nursing had any effect on total fertility, it worked against rather than for the observed fertility differences.

---

21. Eliminated from consideration are all children who died at less than five years of age or who resulted from the last pregnancy preceding the interview. Early death or the interview might have occurred before the end of the normal nursing period of these children.

TABLE V-4

MONTHS NURSING PER CHILD BY SOCIAL BACKGROUND TYPE

Social background type	Number of women	Total fertility rate	Number of women	Children with unlimited nursing*	Months nursing per child
Village, uneducated					
1. Moslem	184	7.43	171	687	18.9
2. Christian	76	8.16	70	348	15.5
City, uneducated					
3. Moslem	136	7.35	123	565	12.0
4. Christian	96	4.14	86	279	11.5
City, educated					
5. Moslem	49	5.56	46	166	10.6
6. Christian	107	3.44	100	242	7.0
TOTAL	648		596**	2,287	

*A child had "unlimited nursing" only if (1) it did not result from the last pregnancy occurring before the interview and (2) it did not die at less than five years of age.

**Fifty two of the women had no child with unlimited nursing by the above definition.

F. Summary

"Involuntary determinants" of fertility are those behaviors which could affect fertility but which do not involve individual intention of affecting fertility. The involuntary determinants studied were age of woman at marriage, frequency of intercourse, periods of prolonged separation from husband, and prolonged nursing of children.

The social background types did not differ appreciably in fecundity, but did display some marked differences in total fertility. Neither prolonged separations nor coital frequency helped to explain these fertility differences. If prolonged nursing had any effect, it would have served to decrease rather than cause the observed fertility differences. By far the major involuntary cause of the observed fertility differences was differential age of woman at marriage.

CHAPTER VI

VOLUNTARY DETERMINANTS OF FERTILITY DIFFERENCES

A. Introduction

"Voluntary determinants" of fertility are actions performed by the couple with the intention of limiting fertility. In short, by "voluntary determinants" we mean birth control. Birth control includes conception control by continence, contraception, or sterilization. It also includes the avoidance of birth after conception by induced abortion.

The present chapter describes the differential birth control behavior employed by the six social background types of our Lebanese sample. The goal is to estimate to what degree differential use of birth control explains the large fertility differences among these social background types.

B. Induced Abortions

1. Introduction

Induced abortions are illegal in Lebanon. Laws forbid propaganda for, selling of facilities for, performing of, and submitting to induced abortion; all carry penalties of both prison and fine. It is doubtful, however, that these laws are widely known or enforced. Although it can be assumed that leaders of all major religious sects discourage induced abortion, probably the most specific stand is the strong one taken by the Catholic church.

In such a situation it would seem difficult indeed to get reliable reports of induced abortions. We attempted to do this by a series of questions. In the process of obtaining a complete history of all the woman's pregnancies, the interviewer found which ones did not end in live birth.   For each of these unsuccessful pregnancies, she asked the woman whether she or anybody else had done anything with the intention of stopping that pregnancy.   What we have, then, is a record of those attempts at induced abortion which the woman admitted and which seemed successful.

2. Differences among Social Background Types

The incidence of induced abortions in a particular social background type can be measured in either of two ways.   One measure is the per cent of the women in the type who had ever induced an abortion.   This measure takes on more meaning if we eliminate women married so briefly that they were less likely to have been tempted to induce abortions; those married less than ten years.   Another measure is the per cent of all pregnancies which ended in induced abortion.[1] Both of these measures are presented in Table VI-1 for each of the social background types.

These results should be interpreted with caution.   Preliminary evaluation of the responses casts far greater doubt upon reports of unsuccessful pregnancies than on reports of live births.[2]   We believe that the errors have resulted mainly in the underestimation of induced abortions[3] for Christian women in the city, whether from educated or uneducated couples (social background types 4 and 6).

Even taking the data at face value we note high rates of ever-use of induced abortion by some social background types.   Almost one-third (31 per cent) of the city Moslem educated couples married ten or more years had attempted one or more induced abortions.

---

1. The resulting per cent should not be interpreted as a measure of the proportion of pregnancies that would end by induced abortion had all women completed their fertile periods.   The large proportion of women who had completed only early parts of their marriages probably cause this figure to be an underestimate for that purpose.
2. See Appendix C: Evaluation of the Data.
3. See Appendix D, Technical Note 1: Possible Errors in Reported Abortions.

TABLE VI-1

PER CENT OF WOMEN EVER INDUCING ABORTION AND PER CENT
OF COMPLETED PREGNANCIES ENDING IN INDUCED ABORTION, BY
SOCIAL BACKGROUND TYPE

Social background types	Total fertility rate*	Number of preg- nancies by all women*	Per cent ending in induced abortion	Number of women married ten or more yrs.	Per cent ever inducing abortion**
Village, uneducated					
1. Moslem	7.43	1,168	0.2	141	2
2. Christian	8.16	512	0.0	58	0
City, uneducated					
3. Moslem	7.35	876	2.5	98	13
4. Christian	4.14	479	7.9	79	20
City, educated					
5. Moslem	5.56	270	13.7	35	31
6. Christian	3.44	413	8.2	69	26

*Based on all 648 women belonging to any social background type.

**Based on those 480 women who belonged to social background types and who had been married ten or more years.

The two measures show almost identical patterns of differences among the social background types. There were almost no induced abortions in the villages. The three least fertile types had by far the highest rates of induced abortion. Induced abortion, then, worked in a direction which might help explain some major fertility differences among the social background types.

3. As an Explanation of Fertility Differences

It is possible to estimate what the total fertility rates of the types would have been had none of the reported induced abortions taken place. One first estimates the time lost through induced abortions, either in waiting for the ill-fated conception, in pregnancy, or in post-partum sterility after the abortion. One then computes corrected total fertility rates using the remaining time only. The corrected total fertility rates should be viewed as rough estimates indeed.[4]

Table VI-2 presents the corrected total fertility rates of the social background types. It also presents the differences between corrected and uncorrected rates.

TABLE VI-2

TOTAL FERTILITY RATES OF SOCIAL BACKGROUND TYPES CORRECTED FOR TIME LOST THROUGH INDUCED ABORTIONS

Social background type	Total fertility rate		
	Uncorrected	Cor-rected	Increase in rate
Village, uneducated			
1. Moslem	7.43	7.45	.02
2. Christian	8.16	8.16	.00
City, uneducated			
3. Moslem	7.35	7.40	.05
4. Christian	4.14	4.27	.13
City, educated			
5. Moslem	5.56	5.88	.32
6. Christian	3.44	3.58	.14

4. The corrected rates assume that induced abortion never caused permanent sterility. There are other sources of error. See Appendix D, Technical Note 4: Correcting for Induced Abortion.

Elimination of induced abortions would have raised especially the fertility of the three least fertile types.[5] However, the degree of increased fertility which would have resulted from eliminating induced abortions was not large: Elimination of induced abortion in the type which had the most induced abortions (educated city Moslems) would have raised the total fertility rate by only 0.32 live births. In short, although induced abortions contributed to some of the major fertility differences, the degree of the contribution probably was small.

4. Inducing Abortion and Contraception

What type of people induce abortions? Two possibilities are suggested: (1) They are unsophisticated couples who lack the foresight or knowledge to control fertility by avoiding pregnancy, and thus must resort to desperate methods after conception. (2) They are sophisticated couples who use a variety of methods for controlling fertility, including both contraception and induced abortion. We can investigate these alternatives by studying the relationship between use of induced abortion and the use of supposedly sophisticated appliance methods of conception control.

From the 801 women married in or after 1920, let us first eliminate those 507 who gave no evidence of any attempt to limit their fertility voluntarily, those women who had never induced an abortion and had never used any method — appliance or non-appliance — to delay any pregnancy.[6] The remaining 294 women all had tried to limit fertility in some way.

---

5. The reader is reminded of our belief that induced abortions were particularly underreported for social background types 4 and 6. If this be so, the corrected total fertility rates of these two types are particularly underestimated.

6. Non-appliance methods included continence, withdrawal and rhythm.

Among these women, the **Q** coefficient of correlation between ever use of appliance methods and ever use of induced abortion was plus .30. Of the 140 women who had ever voluntarily avoided birth in some way, but never by an appliance method, 23 per cent had ever induced an abortion. On the other hand, of the 154 who had ever used an appliance method, 36 per cent also had induced an abortion.

These results do not support the view that abortion inducers were of the unsophisticated type who turned to abortion because they knew of no more sophisticated methods. If anything, they were more likely to have been more sophisticated than the average couple attempting to limit births. It is possible, of course, that couples tended to turn to appliance methods after they had induced an abortion, to avoid the necessity for doing so again.

C. Conception Control

   1. Introduction

Conception control can be achieved by temporary appliance or non-appliance methods, or by permanent sterilization. We will use "non-appliance" methods to mean only continence (total abstinence to conception), withdrawal (coitus interruptus), and safe period (rhythm method).

The effect of conception control practices on the fertility of a class of women is influenced by many factors; the proportion of the women in the class ever using such practices, the point in the marriage when users initiate their attempts, the consistency of their use once they have initiated it, the clinical effectiveness of the methods used, the skill with which the couples use the methods, and others. Among these factors, limitations in time and in the precision of our data allow us to treat only the first two: (1) the proportion of the women in the social background types ever using conception control and (2) the time of initiating conception control.

2. Ever-Use of Conception Control

By limiting our attention to couples who had been married ten or more years, we focus on those couples most likely to have reached a family size where they would have thought of limitation. Table VI-3 presents, for each social background type, the per cent of the couples married ten or more years who had ever used each of the conception control methods.

TABLE VI-3

PER CENT OF WOMEN MARRIED MORE THAN TEN YEARS EVER USING CONCEPTION CONTROL, BY SOCIAL BACKGROUND TYPE

	Village		City			
	Uneducated		Uneducated		Educated	
	Mos.	Chr.	Mos.	Chr.	Mos.	Chr.
Method	1	2	3	4	5	6
	%	%	%	%	%	%
Any Non-Appliance Method	1	14	44	51	51	54
abstinence to delay	0	0	1	0	0	0
withdrawal	1	14	43	51	49	43
safe period	0	2	3	3	9	14
Any Appliance Method	0	0	34	27	60	49
condom	0	0	21	20	54	38
douche (irrigation)	0	0	8	6	9	7
sponge (or cotton tampon, impregnated)	0	0	7	4	9	1
diaphragm (or pessary)	0	0	2	1	6	7
jelly (or suppository)	0	0	6	1	9	1
Other Temporary Method	1	2	11	6	3	6
Sterilization	0	0	1	1	0	10
Any Method	2	16	60	56	83	86
Number of Women	141	58	98	79	35	69

There were marked differences among the social background types. Very small per cents of the village types had ever used any method (2 per cent and 16 per cent). On the other hand, large proportions of all types of city couples had used one or more methods (56 per cent to 86 per cent). In the city, moreover, the educated types were considerably more likely to have used any method than the uneducated types; 83 per cent and 86 per cent as compared with 60 per cent and 56 per cent. There was no apparent consistent difference between the religious classes in their tendency to have used some method or other.

The types of methods favored varied by social background type as well. Those few village couples who ever used any method used non-appliance methods, usually withdrawal. Among the uneducated city dwellers, non-appliance methods were more likely to have been used than appliance methods (44 per cent vs. 34 per cent and 51 per cent vs. 27 per cent). Among the educated city dwellers, on the other hand, the non-appliance methods were matched by appliance methods. Sterilization was used almost solely by the educated city Christians, and then only by ten per cent of the women. In short, with city background the likelihood of ever using a non-appliance method increased, and with education the likelihood of supplementing these methods with appliance methods (and possibly sterilization) increased.[7]

The favorite methods were those involving direct action by the male. Among the non-appliance methods, withdrawal was by far the most popular, abstinence was shunned, and safe period gained prominence

---

7. One might suspect that women who underreport induced abortions also are likely to underreport use of conception control. We believe that the two social background types most probably underreporting induced abortion were the uneducated and educated city Christians, types 4 and 6; See Appendix D, Technical Note 1: Possible Errors in Reported Abortions. We have no way of determining whether these types especially underreported conception control as well.

slightly with education. Among the appliance methods, the condom was by far the most popular, having more users than all of the variety of female methods.

The Catholic position against the use of appliance methods is particularly specific and firm. We have no evidence, however, that Catholics were less inclined to use appliance methods than were Moslems or Orthodox Christians of the same educational and residential background. Among the uneducated city couples, 29 per cent of the Catholics had ever used an appliance method, compared with 34 per cent for the Moslems and 24 per cent for the Orthodox. Among the educated city couples, 49 per cent of the Catholics had ever used such a method, compared with 60 per cent for the Moslems and 50 per cent for the Orthodox. These per cents, however, are based on particularly small numbers of women.[8]

   3. Time of Initiating Conception Control

We will confine our attention again to those women who had been married for ten or more years, and who had ever used conception control. For each of these women we know the first pregnancy she attempted to delay. A summary measure of this timing for any social background type is the median first pregnancy that women attempted to avoid. These medians are presented in Table VI-4. (The reader is cautioned about the small numbers of women represented in the table.)

In general, the least fertile types tended to initiate conception control earliest. Those very few village couples who ever did use any methods used them considerably later on the average than did city couples.

---

8. See Appendix Table F-27.

68

TABLE VI-4

PREGNANCY FIRST DELAYED BY CONCEPTION CONTROL BY
WOMEN MARRIED TEN OR MORE YEARS,
BY SOCIAL BACKGROUND TYPE

Social background type	Total fertility rate *	Number of women ever using conception control **	Median first pregnancy delayed
Village, uneducated			
1. Moslem	7.43	3	—
2. Christian	8.16	9	7.7
City, uneducated			
3. Moslem	7.35	59	4.9
4. Christian	4.14	44	3.6
City, educated			
5. Moslem	5.56	29	3.2
6. Christian	3.44	59	2.4

*Based on the total populations of the social background types, including those married for less than ten years.

**Based only on those women married ten or more years in the social background type.

Among the city couples, the uneducated couples tended to start control more than one pregnancy later than educated couples of the same religious class. Among the Moslems, the median first pregnancy delayed by the uneducated was 4.9 compared with 3.2 for the educated; the parallel figures for the Christians were 3.6 for the uneducated and 2.4 for the educated. In the city, within the education classes, the Moslem couples tended to institute control about one pregnancy later than the Christians; the differences between the medians was 1.3 pregnancies among the uneducated couples and 0.8 among the educated couples. It is worth noting that no Moslem couple reported attempting to delay the first conception. Among the Christians, on the other hand, 4.5 per cent of the controlling uneducated couples and 20.3 per cent of the controlling educated couples reported attempting to delay the first pregnancy.

D. Summary

This chapter has investigated the two main types of methods for voluntarily avoiding birth, (1) preventing the conception and (2) ending the pregnancy by induced abortion. The social background types were found to differ appreciably in their ever use of induced abortion or conception control. In the case of conception control, types were also found to differ in the time of initiating attempts at control and in the methods favored in those attempts. These distinguishing characteristics among the social background types, along with the total fertility rates of the types, are summarized in Table VI-5.

TABLE VI-5

SUMMARY OF MAIN DIFFERENCES IN BIRTH CONTROL BEHAVIOR
AMONG SOCIAL BACKGROUND TYPES

	Village		City			
	Uneducated		Uneducated		Educated	
	Mos.	Chr.	Mos.	Chr.	Mos.	Chr.
Social background type	(1)	(2)	(3)	(4)	(5)	(6)
Total fertility rate	7.43	8.16	7.35	4.14	5.56	3.44
Per cent ever inducing abortion*	2	0	13	20	31	26
Per cent ever using any method of conception control*	2	16	60	56	83	86
Median first pregnancy delayed by conception control*	—	7.7	4.9	3.6	3.2	2.4
Per cent ever using appliance methods of conception control*	0	0	34	27	60	49

*Based on women married ten or more years.

These factors together might explain most of the fertility differences remaining among the social background types after differential age of woman at marriage is taken into account. The high fertility of the villagers was accompanied by almost complete absence of use of either induced abortion or conception control. Although the highly fertile uneducated village Moslems did show an appreciable proportion ever using conception control, they instituted their attempts quite late in marriage. At the other extreme, the very low fertility of the educated city Christians is associated with relatively high proportion ever using induced abortion and conception control, with high proportions using appliance methods, and with earliest use of conception control.

The higher fertility of the educated city Moslems than the uneducated city Christians is not explained by the factors we have analyzed. This points up the possibility of differential underreporting of birth control and the incomplete nature of our analysis of voluntary determinants.

CHAPTER VII

FAMILY SIZE ADVISED

A. Introduction

Voluntary determinants probably were a major cause of fertility differences among social background types of Lebanese women. If this be so, then the goals of this voluntary action become relevant. Although we do not know the family-size goals that motivated couples previous to the interview, we did find their opinions on ideal family size at the time of the interview. We can study these to find what kinds of women were likely to have any specific opinion on family size, and what these opinions were.

B. Opinion Holding

1. Introduction

"Suppose you had a very close friend, in the same circumstances as yourself, and she asked you for advice on the convenient number of children for her. What is the number you would advise her to have, if she could?"

Of the women in our social background types, only 59 per cent were willing to advise specific numbers of children. (Interviewers were instructed to probe with caution.) The refusing women responded with "as God wills," "as many as possible," and similar statements. The very willingness to give specific advice on total family size became a subject of interest.

2. Relation to Social Background Characteristics

Table VII-1 presents, for each social background type, the per cent of women who were willing to advise a specific total number of children to an inquiring friend. The per cent varied widely among

the social background types, ranging from 25 per cent to 90 per cent.
Type of residence seems to have affected this willingness; greater per
cents of <u>city</u> uneducated women were willing (75 per cent and 66 per
cent) than <u>village</u> uneducated women (25 per cent and 43 per cent).
Education also seemed to be a factor; about 90 per cent of the educated
city women offered specific advice.   On the other hand, religion did
not seem to affect this willingness consistently or greatly.

TABLE VII-1
PER CENT OF WOMEN ADVISING ANY SPECIFIC NUMBER OF CHILDREN, BY SOCIAL BACKGROUND TYPE

Social background type	Number of women	Per cent advising specific number of children
Village, uneducated		
1. Moslems	184	25%
2. Christians	76	43
City, uneducated		
3. Moslems	136	75
4. Christians	96	66
City, educated		
5. Moslems	49	90
6. Christians	107	89
TOTAL	648	

3. Relation to Birth Control

    The reader may note that those social background types most
willing to advise specific numbers of children were generally those
most likely to have used any method of birth control.   Furthermore,
among all those women married after 1920 and married for more
than ten years, the association between advising any specific number

of children and ever using any method of birth control was quite high; Q - .73. Of the 378 women who gave specific advice, 64.8 per cent had used birth control; of those 222 women who would advise no specific number, only 22.5 per cent had used birth control.

C. Opinions Expressed

Having been warned that large numbers of women refused to advise on ideal family size, let us turn to the advice offered when offered. Table VII-2 describes the total family size advised by women in each of the social background types.

TABLE VII-2

MEDIAN AND INTERQUARTILE RANGE OF TOTAL CHILDREN
ADVISED BY WOMEN, BY SOCIAL BACKGROUND TYPE

Social background type	Per cent of women advising	Total children advised	
		Median	Inter-quartile range
Village, uneducated			
1. Moslem	26%	4.7	3.7
2. Christian	43	4.1	2.4
City, uneducated			
3. Moslem	75	4.0	1.6
4. Christian	66	4.0	1.3
City, educated			
5. Moslem	90	3.8	1.2
6. Christian	89	3.9	1.3

It seems that the expressed opinions of the social background types were quite similar, save for the village uneducated Moslems. The median family size advised differed so little among the other five types (3.8 to 4.1) that the responses appear to conform to some accepted norm.

74

This is particularly true among the four urban social background types, where the dispersion of responses within any type was quite small. In short, at least those urban women who were willing to advise on specific family size tended to give a stereotyped response of about four children.[1]

D. Summary

Women were asked to give advice on the ideal family size for other women like themselves. A large proportion of women were unwilling to advise any specific number. Willingness to advise a specific number varied widely among the social background types, ranging from 25 per cent to 90 per cent. Previous use of birth control was closely associated with willingness to give such advice.

There was little variation in the number of children advised by those who were willing to advise. At least the city social background types seemed to give a stereotyped response of about four children.

_____

1. The sex ratio advised by the social background types ranged from 1.5 to 1.1 boys per girl. See Appendix F, Table F-28.

CHAPTER VIII

INTERPRETATION

A. <u>The European Demographic Transition</u>

The basic intent of demographic transition theory is (1) to abstract a general pattern of mortality and fertility change in Europe during its modernization and industrial revolution and (2) to use this general pattern as a basis for explaining or predicting mortality and fertility changes in countries now starting their periods of modernization. It may serve as a frame of reference for understanding the observed fertility differences in our sample of Lebanese women.

In its simplest terms, the European transition is seen as one from (1) a state of near balance between high stable fertility and high variable mortality to (2) a state of near balance between low variable fertility and low stable mortality. In the process of transition, mortality is seen to have declined before fertility, causing a period of wide difference between the two, a period of "explosive" growth.

Our interest is in what the pattern suggests for <u>differential</u> fertility within nations during the period of fertility transition. Decline in fertility did not occur simultaneously in all segments of European society. Ryder summarizes the general differences as follows (with apologies for oversimplification):[1]

> "As the occupational structure has gradually been transformed from an agricultural to an industrial focus, those participating most closely in this transformation have modified their fertility downward. By socioeconomic class, the higher the status of the persons concerned, the earlier their fertility decline; the new childbearing pattern has gradually filtered down through the social ranks."

---

1. Ryder, op. cit., p. 412. Ryder finishes his paragraph with the following sentence: "The new style of fertility has met pockets of resistance in subcultures with boundary-maintaining mechanism which are, for the time being at least, relatively effective." The importance of this qualification will become apparent in our discussion of religious effects on fertility differences in Lebanon below.

At any given time, one is likely to have found, in a transitional European society, lower fertility for high socioeconomic status vs. low status urban couples, lower fertility for urban couples vs. rural couples on the same socioeconomic level.

The decline in fertility resulted primarily from the curtailing of large families. In almost all western European countries the curtailment has resulted mainly from voluntary fertility control by married couples. Indeed, the fertility transition is usually seen not only as one from high fertility to low fertility, but also as one from uncontrolled fertility to controlled fertility.

B. Residential and Socioeconomic Differences in Fertility

If Lebanon were in a similar demographic transition, one would expect our sample to show the same residential and socioeconomic fertility differences as those experienced by European countries. One does find the expected pattern, within major religious classes: The total fertility rate of the educated city dwellers was lowest, the fertility of the isolated villagers highest, with the fertility of the uneducated city dwellers somewhere between.

But it is possible that these fertility differences could have been caused by something other than the differential degree of advance toward low fertility of former high fertility classes. This picture of transition in time involves two basic assumptions: (1) the various social background types are differentially involved in transition from one family model to another. (2) The direction of change is from a large family model to a small family model, rather than in the other direction.

We will be in better position to support these assumptions if we can demonstrate (1) that the small family model is not an indigenous one, but rather a modern western one and (2) that the pattern of spread of this model through the classes approximates the pattern one would expect for the spread of any new idea.

The area experts summarized in Chapter I generally support the first point. They agree that the traditional family in Lebanon has been the extended family with many features favoring high and unlimited fertility. They identify the competing system as the western nuclear family model, introduced through contact with Europe and the United States.

Our data also lend support to this point. The challenging western model in its present general form involves post-adolescent marriage of women, the acceptance of a limited family ideal by couples, and the voluntary achievement of limited families through action by couples. The least fertile of our Lebanese social background types tended to marry their women latest, were most willing to advise specific (and limited) family size, were most likely to have used either induced abortion or conception control, and were most likely to have initiated conception control at early parities. The similarity between the modern western model and the behavior of the least fertile types of Lebanese is strong.

With respect to the second point, the expected pattern of spread of most new ideas from outside in most countries would be from the educated city classes to the isolated villagers. This, generally, is the pattern of spread implied by the existing fertility differentials in our sample.

78

Within either religion, then, the three types represented in our sample can be viewed as in different stages of transition from the traditional Lebanese extended family and uncontrolled high fertility to the western-modern nuclear family and controlled low fertility.

C. Religious Differences in Fertility

Within either major religious class, uneducated villagers had the highest fertility and educated city dwellers the lowest. However, the levels of fertility associated with given combinations of residential and socioeconomic background were affected by religious affiliation. Apparently religious identification has qualified how rapidly any residential-socioeconomic type has been making the transition from high fertility to low fertility.

Extremely isolated villagers, whether Christian or Moslem, seem beyond the influence of the new family model. But in the cities the two social background types of Christians seem further along in their transitions than do the corresponding two types of Moslems: Among city residents, the total fertility rates for uneducated and educated Christian types were 4.14 and 3.44, respectively; for the corresponding types of Moslems they were 7.35 and 5.56.

A by product of the religious influence on fertility among city dwellers has been a difference between the patterns of socioeconomic and residential fertility differences for the two major religions. Particularly noteworthy is the near absence of fertility differences at two points where they would be expected: (1) between uneducated village Moslems and uneducated city Moslems, and (2) between uneducated city Christians and educated city Christians.

The lack of rural-urban differences among uneducated Moslems seems best explained by the very early transitional state of uneducated city Moslems. Certainly the uneducated city Moslems seem earlier in their transition than do their Christian counterparts. Their total fertility rate was higher, 7.35 compared with 4.14. Their women married at earlier average ages, 17.9 compared with 21.2. They were less likely to have induced abortion. Although they were not less likely to have used conception control, they initiated control more than one pregnancy later on the average. To the degree that they lagged behind their Christian counterparts in transition to lower controlled fertility one would expect them to more closely approximate the fertility of (presumably pre-transitional) villagers.

The explanation for the very small fertility difference between uneducated and educated city Christians is more complex. One could argue that further fertility declines of a given absolute size would be more difficult among classes already low in fertility than in classes still high in fertility. A reduction in total fertility rate of one live birth would represent only a 12 per cent decrease for the uneducated village Christians (with a present total fertility rate of 8.16) but would represent a 29 per cent decrease for the educated city Christians (with a present total fertility rate of 3.44). As women lower their fertility, they tend to increase the proportion of their married lives spent non pregnant and in risk of further conception. The average desired family size of any class probably is not zero, but some value above that. As fertility reaches the desired level for increasing proportions of couples in a class, increasing proportions of couples will not contribute additional contraceptive efforts to bring their fertility to a yet lower point.   In short, as class fertility gets low, the resistances to further decline increase.

If this be true, then the recent fertility decline of the least fertile social background type (the educated city Christians) may have been slower than the recent fertility decline of the next to least fertile type (the uneducated city Christians).   The difference between their total fertilities would tend to decrease as the absolute level of fertility of the least fertile class got lower and lower.   This would imply that the present fertility difference between uneducated and educated city Christians has been larger, but has been decreasing lately.[2]

Our analysis leaves unanswered the question why city Christians might make the transition to the limited family model more readily than city Moslems, even within the same educational classes. Some possible explanations are recorded in Chapter I.   Lebanon is a plural society in which religious sects have had rather separate histories and different outside affiliations in the past and present.   The Christian sects have had closer identification with Europe and the United States in the past and present than have the Moslems; thus the avenues for the transmission of the western family model have been better for the Christians than for the Moslems.   The general rationality of the western-oriented Christians, as contrasted with Moslem fatalism, would predispose the former more to planning of any type, including family planning.

---

2. This explanation would imply that at an earlier period larger socioeconomic differences in fertility did exist among city Christians. Our analysis of the older generation in our sample is inconclusive on this point. However, it is interesting to note that Rizk did find larger socioeconomic differences among Christians in Egyptian cities than we did in Lebanese cities. Egypt is generally considered less advanced in modernization than Lebanon. (The existence of this socioeconomic differential among city Christians in Egypt but not in Lebanon was the only major discrepancy between the differentials reported for Egypt and for Lebanon.)

The frame of reference used in this explanation pictures a religion as a social group or sect having a particular position in a society, particular relations with other internal and external groups, and a peculiar social history. An alternate frame of reference views the religion as a set of ethical principles, preserved and specified in the sacred literature, and interpreted through the hierarchy of religious officials.

The second frame of reference has been of little help in explaining religious fertility differentials in Lebanon. Unable to conclude that the specific doctrines of any major religious sect were particularly permissive of fertility control, we had no basis for explaining differential fertility control by members of the various sects. The one case in which there was a specific doctrine — the Catholic one forbidding use of appliance methods — it bore no apparent relation to the actual behavior of the sect. Moslem permission of polygyny and easy divorce did not prove to relate to the major religious fertility differentials discovered.

D. Future Fertility Differences

One can speculate what this interpretation implies for the near future of fertility differentials in Lebanon. Among the Christians, one would expect (1) a further decrease in the already small socio-economic fertility differences in the city and, accordingly, (2) an increase in the difference between uneducated city dwellers and uneducated isolated villagers. Among the Moslems, one would expect (1) a continued decrease in the fertility of both educated and uneducated city dwellers and, accordingly, (2) an increase in the fertility differences between uneducated city dwellers and uneducated isolated villagers, then finally (3) a decrease in the socioeconomic fertility differences in the city.

In the more distant future, one might expect the villages as well to start the transition to the limited family model. But what to expect ultimately of city fertility is not suggested by demographic transition theory. After all city classes have brought fertility under voluntary control, then fertility will reflect the choices of the partners at the time, just as it does at present in urban United States.

APPENDIX A

THE SAMPLE

1. Attrition and Bias

a. The Population

In the context of sampling, bias results from sampling a population other than that one claims to be representing. The term has meaning only when one specifies the population one is attempting to represent.

We cannot claim to represent the national population of Lebanon. Nor can we claim to represent all women who would have been interviewed by the sampling procedure had no women been lost by death and emigration between their marriages and the interview. Death and emigration probably were selective by social background. It is impossible to guess what the fertility of these lost women would have been had they not died or emigrated. In short, we can represent only the survivors of marriage cohorts.

The most defensible population for us to consider would be the following: all women who would have been interviewed had we continued choosing cases indefinitely by the specified sampling procedure. This is an admittedly vague definition, due our purposive selection of units. It is used here only to organize our discussion of bias.

b. Possible Sources of Bias

The analysis reported in the text consists of comparisons among social background classes with respect to fertility and behavior which could have affected fertility. Comparative statements could be biased if (1) the women lost from a given social background class were different from the women remaining in that class with respect to fertility or fertility-determining behavior, and (2) the proportion of women lost from any given social background class was appreciable. Attrition resulted from refusals and from elimination of incomplete or grossly inconsistent interview schedules. "Refusals" are defined as (1) "total refusals" (a) who were contacted but who refused the interview or (b) who could not be contacted, and (2) "cut-offs" who started the interview but did not finish it. The few interview schedules which were brought in as complete, but later found incomplete and uncompletable, were classified as "cut-offs."[1]

Of the 1,037 interviews attempted, 12.3 per cent were refused or cut off. The refusal rate in Beirut was 11.9 per cent; the rate in villages was 13.2 per cent.

Urban interviewers were questioned later about the general types of women who had refused them. Rural interviewers

---

[1] We are fairly sure of full reporting of refusals. Interviewers were financially rewarded for both refused and cut-off interviews. They reported these every time they turned in a set of completed interviews.

were asked later to describe each woman who refused them. Interviewers' descriptions of women refusing them were, of course, guesses.

Our conclusion would be (1) that social-background classes varied somewhat in their refusal rates but (2) that the women refusing from the classes had no suspected differences in fertility from those who did not refuse in that class. In short, no bias is apparent from the refusals.

One word of caution. Interviewers did report that women with no children were slightly more likely to refuse than women with some children. However, they did not indicate that this basis of refusal followed any particular social background lines. Therefore, we cannot determine that this constituted a source of bias in inter-class comparisons. Rather we must assume that it caused very slight overestimates of the fertility of every class.[2]

Twenty eligible cases were eliminated before the analysis because they had incomplete information on marital history or proved highly inconsistent in their information on duration of marriage. Most of these cases were older women who would not have been included in the central tabulations of the analysis even had they not been discarded. None of the

---

[2] Appendix D, Technical Note 2 reports that social background types did not vary appreciably in the proportion of respondents judged infecund.

cases which would have been used was sterile. The eliminated
cases would have been about proportionately distributed among
social background classes defined by religion and type of
residence. We conclude that preliminary elimination of cases,
like refusals, presents no known threat of bias.

2. Social Background Characteristics of the Sample

a. Communities Interviewed

The city of Beirut is by far the major city in Lebanon
and in the immediate region. The population of the metropolitan
district at the time of the interviewing probably was over 400,000
and perhaps this could be increased by 50% if one refers to the
whole metropolitan area of which it is the center. Beirut serves
as an entrepot not only for Lebanon, but also for Syria and
Jordan. It is the center of political life, culture, education,
and Western contact in Lebanon.[3] All of the women interviewed
in Beirut lived rather close to the city center.

The two villages were chosen to represent the other
extreme on the rural-urban continuum from Beirut. They were
neighboring villages, situated in the northern Bekaa valley,
across the Lebanon mountain range from the seacoast and the large
cities. Ainata is approximately 56 miles from Beirut; Chaate
is approximately 48 miles from Beirut. The closest town to
either is Baalbek, about 18 miles from Ainata and 9 miles from

---

[3]A 1953 social survey of Beirut is recorded in Churchill, op.
cit.

Chaate on roads passable by automobile. Both villages are
served by buses to nearby larger villages. The population of
Ainata was about 800; the population of Chaate was about 2,000.
Both villages, then, are very small and very isolated.

They are approximately equivalent in terms of economic
development, though the smaller Ainata could be considered as
having a slight advantage. Both consist almost wholly of
farmers, mainly small landholders. In both subsistence agri-
culture is mixed with farming of cash crops. In both there
is an elementary school but no higher education in the village.
Of the two, Ainata probably uses slightly more irrigation and
has a slightly lower proportion of landless farm laborers.

The important distinction between the villages is
in religious affiliation. Ainata is virtually all Maronite
Catholic. Chaate is about equally split between Sunni and
Shiite Moslems.

   b. Classification by Residence, Education, and Religion

The sampling method resulted in a sample rather
closely approximating the composition dictated by the study
design. Table A-1 shows, for the 873 accepted respondents,
the composition by type of residence during the first five
years after marriage, by religious sect of the husband, and
by the highest education attained by either member of the
couple.

89

Table A-1

Religious, Residential, and Educational Background of the Total Sample

Residence of Couples after Marriage and Religious Sect of Husband	Highest Education Attained by Either Member of Couple				
	Illiterate	Literate	Elementary Certificate	Lebanese Brivet or Higher	Tot
	(1)	(2)	(3)	(4)	(5
City					
Sunnite	29	89	41	43	20
Shiite	12	19	3	3	3
Druze	1	6	0	5	1
Total Moslem	42	114	44	51	25
Maronite Catholic	2	44	12	29	8
Other Catholic	1	15	13	36	6
Orthodox	9	41	7	41	9
Protestant	0	0	0	3	
Total Christian	12	100	32	109	25
Town or Village					
Sunnite	39	33	2	4	7
Shiite	93	48	1	6	14
Druze	1	1	1	0	
Total Moslem	133	82	4	10	22
Maronite Catholic	42	61	3	6	11
Other Catholic	2	4	1	4	1
Orthodox	1	10	2	3	1
Protestant	0	1	0	0	
Total Christian	45	76	6	13	14

All major religious sects are represented in both
the city and the town-or-village classes; the main deficiency
is in town-or-village Orthodox couples. Among the city residents, both Christians and Moslems are rather widely spread on
education. Town-or-village couples included very few who had
ever received an elementary educational certificate.

c. Other Characteristics of the Classes

The basic classes used in the analysis proper are
those based on combinations of type of residence after marriage,
highest education of the couple, and religion of the husband.
The other known characteristics of these basic classes are
summarized here. Tables describing distributions on these
other characteristics are filed in Appendix F.

Year of marriage. The better-educated classes tended
to have been married more recently than the less-educated
classes. Among the city Moslems, 54.7 per cent of the illiterate
couples were married after 1939 while 74.5 per cent of the couples
with Lebanese Brivet or higher degree were married after 1939.
The analogous figures for the Christians were 33.3 per cent and
70.6 per cent. This, of course, would be the expected result
of a continuous spread of formal education.[4]

Pre-marital history of the women. The interview
schedule gathered information on the education of the woman
as well as her husband, the woman's main occupation before

---

[4]See Appendix F, Table F-29.

91

marriage, and her number of living siblings at marriage.

There is the expected close relation between the education of women and the education of their husbands. However, the basic classes differ in the degree to which the women's education approximates that of their husbands, when the husbands had any education. Specifically, Christian women tend to have education closer to that of their husbands than do Moslem women; city women tend to have education closer to that of their husbands then do town or village women.[5]

Women were asked questions to determine if they had ever worked for money during the last five years before marriage and, if so, whether their best-paying position during that period involved work mostly away from home. Apparently city Christian women, regardless of education, were more likely to have had pre-marital away-from-home paid occupational experience than were either Moslem city women or noncity women of either religion.[6]

Women were asked how many living siblings they had at the time they were married. There was little variation among the mean number of living siblings for the basic classes. The range was from 4.0 (for educated noncity Christians), with all of the other means falling between 4.4 and 4.6.[7]

---

[5] See Appendix F, Table F-30.

[6] See Appendix F, Table F-31.

[7] See Appendix F, Table F-32.

<u>Residence History</u>. The basic residence classification
refers to the couple during the first five years after marriage.
We have, in addition, the main type of residence of both the
woman and her husband-to-be during the last five years before
marriage, and the place of interview of the woman.[8]

Among the couples living in the city immediately
after marriage, there was very little variation in residence
history. Between 83% and 100% of the husbands had lived in
cities immediately previous to marriage, depending on education
class. The Moslem women were slightly more likely to have come
from city premarital residences than were Christian women, but
the least urban class of women still had 67% of its women living
in cities immediately before marriage. In short, there was a
history of predominant urban residence before marriage for all
post-marital city residents, and very little variation among
the education-religion classes in the degree to which this was
so. Finally, virtually all of the women classified as city
immediately after marriage were interviewed in the city, and
presumably had lived there since their marriages.

The consistency between pre- and post-marital residence is high among the couples living in towns or villages
during the first five years after marriage. Very little urban
to rural migration seems to have taken place about the time of
marriage. The striking exception to this generalization is

---

[8]See Appendix F, Table F-33.

mong the well-educated couples in both religions living in
:owns or villages after marriage. A majority of these couples
had lived in the city previous to marriage, and were later
interviewed in the city. This, of course, casts doubt upon
the identification of these better-educated couples as noncity, and supports their elimination from the social background
types.

Post-marital economic status. The highest education
level attained by either member of the couple is used as the
central measure of the socio-economic status of the couple
throughout the analysis proper. However, we do have other
information about the economic achievement of the couple after
marriage. Although this information is probably less reliable
than the information on education, we can use it at least to
get a fuller picture of what given levels of education seemed
to mean about the later economic achievement of the couple.

One measure of post-marital economic status was the
rooms per capita in the main residence during the first five
years after marriage.[9] As might be expected, education of the
couple is quite closely related to the later housing conditions
the couple enjoyed. Within either the city or the town or
village, the median rooms per capita rises consistently with

---

[9] In obtaining this quotient, a count was taken of the age of
the people. People aged 0 to 9 were counted as one-third; people
aged 11 to 19 were counted as two-thirds; people aged 20 or over
were counted as full persons. The sum of these people who slept
in the dwelling unit was divided into the total non-storage rooms
in the dwelling unit.

the level of education attained by the couple. However, within any given education class, the Christian couples had a slightly higher record of rooms per capita than the Moslems. Thus, city illiterate Moslems had 0.8 rooms per capita as compared with 1.0 for city illiterate Christians; city Moslems of the highest education class had a median of 1.8 rooms per capita while Christians in that class had a median of 2.1 rooms per capita.[10]

The _occupation_ by which the husband earned most of his yearly income during the first five years after marriage was determined and classified by a series of questions. As one would expect, among the city dwellers the type of occupation was quite closely related to the highest education of the couple. The professions and clerical positions were filled almost entirely by men with at least elementary educational certificates and usually higher degrees. The commercial and industrial positions and skilled work or crafts, on the other hand, displayed a curvilinear relationship with education, drawing mainly from couples who had elementary certificates and less from couples having either higher or lower education. Unskilled workers or servants and non-self-supporting people came predominantly from illiterate couples and drew progressively less from better-educated classes.

---

[10] See Appendix F, Table F-34.

Approximately the same pattern of relationship
between education and urban occupation applied to both religious groups. However, a higher proportion of poorly educated
Moslems than Christians were either non-self-supporting or
employed as unskilled workers or servants. Similarly, Moslems
with educational degrees were slightly more likely to take
commercial or industrial positions - as contrasted with professional or clerical - when compared with Christians of the
same educational levels. But these residual religious differences were quite small.[11]

Not all of the town-or-village residents earned most
of their living by themselves farming. Even among the illiterate
couples about 20% of both the Moslems and the Christians had as
their main source of income some non-farming occupation. This
proportion, of course, grew with education. Among those very
few who had elementary certificates or higher degrees, about
90% had nonfarm main occupations, the largest category being
the professions. In both religions, the majority of the farmers
owned some land.

_____

[11] See Appendix F, Table F-35.

96

APPENDIX B

TECHNICAL NOTES ON GATHERING THE DATA

This appendix records that part of our field experience which might be useful to researchers planning similar
surveys in similar areas. The emphasis is on practices peculiar
to surveys in developing countries and on intimate subjects.
When possible, we attempt to give some ex post facto evaluation
of the techniques we have used.[1]

1. The Research Staff

a. Research Assistants

As in other surveys, it was necessary that research
assistants be accomplished in the general skills of social
research. In addition, however, this study required that they
be fluent both in the language of the unilingual project director
and in that of the area in which the field work was to take place.
Furthermore, their knowledge of the area of study had to be great
in order to compensate for the ignorance of the project director.
We found Lebanese graduate students in sociology at the American
University of Beirut to be qualified for this demanding role.
Their only possible limitation was their apparent youth, which
they had to overcome in commanding respect in some of their roles.

Research assistants were valuable at all stages of
the field work, from designing the interview schedule to coding
the results. In designing the schedule they were able to furnish

---

[1]
For a more thoroughgoing evaluation of a similar experience, see
Kurt W. Back and J. Mayone Stycos, The Survey under Unusual Con-
ditions: Methodological Facets of The Jamaica Human Fertility
Investigation. Monograph Number 1, 1959 published by the Society
for Applied Anthropology, 52 pp.

the project director with the likely frame of reference of the respondents, the meaning of questions to them, the likely limits of rapport and memory. After the schedule had been drafted in English, the research assistants were able to see to its translation into Lebanese Arabic.

The project director could train the interviewers in the use of the English version of the interview schedule. But in the use of the final local-language version, only skilled interviewers knowing the local language could train. Qualified research assistants performed this function as well.

The reliance on research assistants was greatest in the field. They served as interpreters and guides to the project director as he visited the areas to be interviewed to gain local rapport. They helped make arrangements for travel, rooming, etc. They accompanied the interviewers to the field in those cases where the presence of a foreigner might have raised suspicion. Finally, they handled all the immediate editing of completed schedules, since all were in Arabic.

After the data were gathered, they supervised the translation and codification of Arabic responses into a form understandable to the project director.

In short, research assistants were required to do some tasks not usually necessary in domestic surveys and also some tasks which the project director himself could do in domestic studies. Their importance can hardly be exaggerated.

b. Liaison Workers

   The project director, being a relative outsider,
needed others to assist him in establishing close contacts with
the area in which the study was to take place. Two ladies were
found who were known and respected in medical and social work
circles in Lebanon, had existing contacts with possible local
sponsors and personnel, and had full understanding and agree-
ment with the goals of the study. These ladies were essential
at the initial stage of recruiting interviewers and approaching
potential sponsors. But their service as a communication link
between the project director and all others concerned continued
throughout the field phase.

c. Interviewer Selection

   It was considered essential that the interviewers be
women, that they be available for work throughout the scheduled
interviewing periods, that they have full command of English as
well as written Arabic and Lebanese colloquial spoken Arabic,
and that they appear mature and competent to female respondents.
We were delighted if we also found previous experience in interviewing in such a woman. We tried to avoid selecting women who
had strong biases about the subject matter of the study and who
might be tempted to educate the respondents or express these
biases. We made sure to have interviewers of all major religious
sects.

Only two experienced interviewers were found by contacting directors of previous studies. The majority were located by our liaison workers from among teachers and social workers. Two more were graduate students in sociology from the American University of Beirut whom the project director felt were likely to have the basic qualifications.

The screening procedure was not highly formalized. The project director did hold an initial interview with each applicant, and performed an initial screening then. The central procedure for subsequent screening was to insist upon high standards of performance and to depend upon discouragement of those unable to meet the standards as a method of elimination. Interviewers were tested in the training periods, evaluated on the basis of the pretest, and constantly corrected by editors throughout both the urban and the rural phases of interviewing. Nine women did the final interviewing in Beirut and twelve in the villages.

We are not prepared to give specific advice on the characteristics of good interviewers. Any generalization we might make would be contradicted by our own experience.

d. Interviewer Training

Most of the interviewers were associated with the project for a full year. During that time, they had a chance to gain paid training and to accumulate experience. First they were subjected to a full week of training, the content of which is described below. A few months later (after the Lebanese insurrection of 1958) most of them were given a refresher training period, then supervised in a field pretest. Finally, previous to the final field work, the survivors were given a few more days of supervised practice. Over this long period, we made every attempt to help them identify themselves with the project and with the role of skilled interviewer.

The initial training week was the most complete. The first three days were taken up by lectures on the design of the study, the place of interviewing in the study, basic principles of interviewing, fundamentals of female fertility, the fertility of Lebanese women, the importance of the study, problems of interviewing women, and problems of interviewing in Lebanon. We were lucky to have these lectures presented by a variety of experts, including two women doctors, the regional United Nations expert on demographic and social statistics, and a social researcher experienced in the area. These lectures were not only informative, but also gave the trainees some feeling of importance in what they were undertaking.

The last two days of this week, and the subsequent refresher training periods, consisted mainly of supervised practice. In these periods, we worked progressively from training to practice. We started with demonstration interviews, with all trainees recording the responses on practice schedules. Discussion of this demonstration interview clarified many fine

points on interviewing skill. Correction of the recorded interview schedules assured clear understanding of their meaning.
Next, trainees practiced on each other in small groups which
included a skilled supervisor to correct errors in technique.
In these small group practices, trainees first mastered the
English schedule, then practiced on the Arabic schedule. Finally,
trainees paired off to practice using the Arabic schedule until
they felt fully competent.

We feel that this rather exhaustive training sequence
was necessary for several reasons: first, it served to identify
the woman with the role of interviewer in an important study,
and built up motivation. Second, it allowed group morale to
develop. Third, it allowed the trainee to develop a confidence
in her skill, which she would find essential in the field. All
of these results were in addition to the central function of
teaching interviewing skills.

2. Gaining Rapport

Our Lebanese advisors were skeptical about the possibility of this survey. They feared that the subject matter
demanded a level of rapport impossible to gain in short interviews. Their fears motivated us to take extreme precautions
to insure maximum rapport.

a. Practices Employed

The main technique was to get visible evidence of
sponsorship by respected groups and individuals in Lebanon.

The relevant groups in Lebanon were individual doctors, social work organizations, and people associated with education in these fields. We took care to represent all major religious groups in our sponsors. Of the 17 potential sponsors approached, 16 were willing to commit themselves immediately to written support.

The project director or a liaison worker visited each potential sponsor armed with a written statement of the objectives and method of the study. He would answer any questions which the potential sponsor might have. If the sponsor wished to be associated with the study, he was asked to sign a prepared simple Arabic statement to that effect on each of twenty small cards. These cards were later distributed among the interviewers for them to show at their discretion in opening interviews.

Armed with this evidence of local support, we were in a position to ask permission from the government. The Ministry of Social Affairs was cooperative enough to supply each interviewer with an identification card legitimizing her role to respondents and local officials.

Before interviewing in the villages, we took two additional steps. First we obtained an additional sponsorship card from the public health doctor serving the area. And second, we made preliminary visits to the village headmen to explain the study and get their cooperation.

In interviewer training, the women practiced the
opening of the interview and gaining rapport. The written
instructions to interviewers quoted below describe the general
approach:

"Establishing rapport is best accomplished by (a)
immediately identifying yourself and justifying your presence
and (b) convincing the woman of the importance of her cooperation.

"(a) The easiest way to identify yourself is to
show the woman your identification card from the Ministry of
Social Affairs (or mention some local leader who has prepared
the women for your visit, if this is the case).

"(b) Getting the woman's cooperation may be best
accomplished by stating the content of the following statement at this point:

'A group of doctors have decided that they need
to know more about Lebanese couples and their children. They
need to know how many children Lebanese couples have, and what
problems couples meet in taking care of these children. They
need this information to give better advice when couples ask
for it.

'These doctors believe that only Lebanese wives can
tell them what they need to know. So they have sent me, and
several other Lebanese women, to ask some questions.

'This has nothing to do with the government, although
the Ministry of Social Affairs has tried to help the doctors
in gathering the facts.

'The doctors do not want the names of the women. No
one, not even the doctors, will know who gave what facts.'

"If the woman asks 'what doctors,' show the sponsorship cards you think appropriate for that particular woman.
Read off the names if it appears that the woman cannot read."

Field assignments, as well, were planned to maximize
the possibility of rapport. It was guessed, correctly, that
the main danger to rapport would come through the spreading of

104

rumors about the intentions of the interviewer among the respondents. The role of survey interviewer is not an established one in Lebanon, and her presence immediately becomes the subject of speculation. The techniques for avoiding such rumors varied with the type of community.

In Beirut, we used the approach of letting the potential respondents in an area become familiar with a particular interviewer. Each interviewer was assigned a block or set of blocks to which she returned daily. She took time to make acquaintance with curious neighbors, to explain the study, and to make appointments for future interviews.

In the villages, logistic considerations - among others - made this technique impractical. Instead we attempted to outdistance the rumors by doing all interviewing in a village within a single day. (As mentioned above, we also legitimized interviewing on that day through the village headman.)[2]

b. <u>Degree of Success</u>

The overall refusal rate was lower than all <u>a priori</u> guesses; 12.3%. This refusal rate includes not only interviews totally refused, but also those cut off after initiation, those which were not started because a known respondent could not be contacted after repeated attempts, and interviews incompletely recorded. In short, not all refusals can be attributed to lack of rapport.

---

[2]
The effectiveness of this technique can be illustrated by negative example. In the village where we had to return to finish on a second day, we were met by unusual uncooperativeness.

The type of woman most likely to refuse varied with the community, according to interviewers' reports. Among the Beirut women, the rich Christian women seemed most likely to refuse, using their maids as barriers from the public. In the villages, older women seemed more likely to refuse, mainly out of unwillingness to be bothered. A few Moslem village women were alienated by rumors of the very intimate questions and refused on the basis of modesty. In addition, some Sunni Moslem women refused on the basis of misconceived political intent of the study. What is notable from the interviewers' reports is that the intimate subject of inquiry was the basis for only a small proportion of the refusals.[3]

This contention is supported by the observation that once a woman had initiated the interview, she was not likely to refuse even the most intimate questions. By far the most refused question was that on frequency of intercourse during the first year after marriage; 8.3% of women married before 1929 refused and 4.6% of married in or after 1929 refused. There were almost no refusals to any other question.

---

[3]The possible bias resulting from attrition is discussed in Appendix A, part 1.

3. Unusual Formal Features of the Interview Schedule

a. Language of the Questions.

In the pretest version of the interview schedule we used the best written approximation of Lebanese colloquial Arabic for all questions. The interviewers found some of the questions extremely hard to use in this form. Questions asking for precise facts became quite complicated in colloquial language, and were confusing to the respondent. The variations in colloquial language within Lebanon were great enough to make the wording inappropriate for respondents in some areas. As a result, interviewers found that they had to reword questions sometimes in order to communicate clearly. Viewing this uncontrolled rewording as intolerable, we decided upon a special policy for the wording of questions in the final schedule: questions referring to facts about the woman's history were in the form of classical Arabic statements describing exactly the facts requested. The interviewer was instructed to use her own words in describing the required fact to the respondent, but to make very sure that she was getting exactly the right fact. Classical rather than colloquial Arabic was used to describe the fact because the former is a more precise written language.

Questions referring to opinions or feelings, on the other hand, were written in Lebanese colloquial Arabic, in quotation marks. Interviewers were instructed to ask these questions verbatim, and to avoid altering the question wording in probing.

b. Degree of Structuring

      The questions in the interview schedule were struc-
tured to an unusually high degree. All responses were to be
recorded in the form of numbers, code numbers, or check marks.
Even possible responses to opinion questions were precoded on
the basis of the pretest results. As a precaution, space was
provided for the interviewer to record details of responses
which were not easily classifiable; these were then classified
in the editing process in conference with a research assistant
and the project director.

      The reason for this apparently premature structuring
of questions was the language problem. Number and check answers
could be understood by the project director by referring to his
English translation of the blank interview schedule; Arabic
word answers could not.

      If the main content of the interview schedule had
been the attitudes and opinions of the respondents, this struc-
turing would have been limiting indeed. But the emphasis rather
was on clearly defined facts. Although the central data probably
were not harmed by this technique, it is probable that the worth
of opinion questions was limited by it.[4]

---

[4]See Appendix C, Evaluation of the Data.

APPENDIX C

EVALUATION OF THE DATA

1. Introduction

      Previous to the analysis reported in the text, we evaluated the data to find the relative reliability and validity of responses to the various questions in the interview schedule. These findings do not represent firm conclusions, but rather best guesses from limited clues. Nevertheless, such guesses were useful in deciding which data to depend on heavily in the analysis and which to ignore, how much precision to expect, and how to allow for error.

      The findings are summarized here primarily for the information of anyone else anticipating the use of similar questions on similar populations.

2. Basis of Evaluation

      Conclusions on relative accuracy of responses were based on several sources of partial information. Interviewer comments on the subject were solicited both immediately after the urban interviewing and the rural interviewing. Partial reinterviews were obtained for six urban respondents and six rural respondents, not randomly selected. Several consistency checks were built into the interview schedule. The face validity of some responses was evaluated on the basis of the plausibility of responses or distributions of responses. A high proportion of refusals or "don't know" responses to a question cast the other responses to that question into doubt. Reliable independent data usable for validation were not available.

3. Relative Accuracy of Variables

The variables resulting from the interview schedule
can be classified into (a) social background characteristics,
(b) pregnancy histories, (c) immediate determinants of fertility, and (d) knowledge and attitudes. In general, we judge
the relative accuracy of these classes of variables to follow
the order in which they are presented above.

a. Social Background Characteristics

If we were to rank the subclasses of characteristics
from most reliably to least reliably measured, the order would
be as follows: (1) religion, (2) education, (3) type of residence, (4) rooms per capita, and (5) occupation of husband.

Within each of these categories of characteristics,
there seems to have been relative inaccuracy following this
pattern: Reports on characteristics of the husband were less
accurate than reports on the characteristics of the woman herself. Statements about periods after marriage tended to be
more reliable than statements about pre-marital periods.

b. Pregnancy Histories

Pregnancy histories included descriptions of all
pregnancies, whether ending in live birth, still birth, spontaneous abortion, or induced abortion. Generally, the rate of
omissions of pregnancies from reports seemed quite low. Live
births probably were most completely reported, still births

next, and spontaneous or induced abortions least completely.[1]
Women with many pregnancies were more likely to forget pregnancies, and particularly those pregnancies which ended in
spontaneous or induced abortions.

The pregnancy history recorded not only the occurrence
of vital events, but also the time of these events relative to
the date of marriage. We conjecture that reports of time of
pregnancy very seldom deviated from the truth by more than one
year. We found no evidence that the errors were non-random in
nature.

c. Immediate Determinants

Although women seemed more accurate in reporting
their own ages at marriage than those of their husbands, they
gave evidence of rounding even their own ages to numbers ending
in 0 and 5. Questions on frequency of intercourse elicited
more refusals than any other questions. Although some unbeliev-
ably high rates of intercourse were reported, the expected decrease in frequency during marriage was reported. Reports of
ever use of contraceptive methods probably were more accurate
than reports of use by pregnancy interval; reports on success
or failure of methods were judged almost worthless. We were
unable to evaluate reports on periods of absence or abstinence.
In responding to questions on periods of nursing for specific
children, women probably tended to arrive at some average nursing
period for themselves and to report this for every child. In

---

[1] See Appendix D, Technical Note 1: Possible Errors in Reported
Abortions.

general, summary statements about total pregnancy histories
or large parts thereof probably were more reliable than
reports about specific pregnancy intervals.

4. Relative Accuracy of Respondents

The longer the woman had been married by the time of
the interview, the more likely she was to give vague information,
to omit reference to events, or to refuse to respond to intimate
questions. This was true on all questions referring to social
background immediately before or after marriage. It also was
true of particularly intimate questions, such as those on frequency of intercourse or use of contraception.

The more pregnancies a woman had had, the more
inaccurate her memory of her pregnancy history. She was more
likely to forget pregnancies, especially unsuccessful ones.
She also was less sure of the time when remembered events
occurred.

APPENDIX D

TECHNICAL NOTES ON THE ANALYSIS

1. Possible Errors in Reported Abortions

a. Reported Rates

In the process of obtaining the history of all pregnancies for each woman, the result of the pregnancy was classified as live birth, spontaneous abortion, still birth, or induced abortion. If the child was not alive at the moment of birth, the woman was asked whether she or anybody else had done anything with the intention of ending the pregnancy unsuccessfully; if she answered "yes," then the result was classified an induced abortion. Issues which were dead but which were not induced abortions were classified into spontaneous abortions and still births on the basis of the woman's estimate of her duration of pregnancy at issue; all unsuccessful pregnancies seven months or longer were classified as still births, the remainder as spontaneous abortions. The per cents of the total completed pregnancies by women in each social background type reported to have ended in spontaneous or induced abortions are presented in Table D-1.[1]

Preliminary evaluation of the reports on unsuccessful pregnancies leads us to suspect a relatively high degree of error

---

[1] These social background types were used in investigating the immediate determinants of fertility differences. For the definition of the types, see Chapter IV.

TABLE D-1

PER CENT OF PREGNANCIES ENDING SPONTANEOUS AND INDUCED ABORTIONS, BY SOCIAL BACKGROUND TYPE

Social background type	Number of pregnancies	Abortions		Total
		Spontaneous	Induced	
Village, uneducated				
1. Moslem	1168	10.4%	0.2%	10.6%
2. Christian	512	10.0	0.0	10.0
City, uneducated				
3. Moslem	876	11.1	2.5	13.6
4. Christian	479	14.8	7.9	22.7
City, educated				
5. Moslem	270	7.4	13.7	21.1
6. Christian	413	13.8	8.2	22.0

in these responses.[2/] Therefore, we should inspect the reports recorded in Table D-1 for plausibility. Some doubtful patterns appear.

Spontaneous abortion rates are markedly higher among the city Christians than among other types. They are higher than among villagers. They are considerably higher than among city Moslems of the same education class.

The total abortion rate is markedly higher among the last three types than among the first three. And among these last three (uneducated city Christians, educated city Moslems, and educated city Christians) there is little variation among the total abortion rates. But the proportion of these total abortions claimed to have been induced is much higher among

------

[2/] See Appendix C: Evaluation of the Data.

the educated city Moslems than among the city Christians, educated or
uneducated.

b. Possible Sources of Error

We are made aware of one major source of error by the comments of interviewers and the analysis of reinterviews. Women were
more likely to forget to report unsuccessful pregnancies than successful
pregnancies. Moreover, the women most likely to have made such
omissions were found to be the women who had been pregnant most often.
Since the classes with the highest reported fertility were likely to include higher proportions of women having had many pregnancies, the
most fertile classes were most likely to have underestimated rates of
unsuccessful pregnancies.

Another source of error might be the reluctance to admit that
a given abortion was induced. To the degree that this reluctance was
typical of any social background type, the proportion of abortions called
spontaneous might be spuriously increased and the proportion of abortions called induced might be spuriously reduced.

On the other hand, where no shame is attached to induced abortion it is possible to overestimate the per cent of abortions induced. An
abortion was classed "induced" if the woman admitted that anyone did
anything with the intention of ending the pregnancy. Spontaneous abortions preceded by such action might be classed as induced even if the
action had nothing to do with the abortion.

c. Likely Effect of These Errors

Our best guesses about the nature and direction of error resulting from these three sources are as follows: The first source of

error, tendency to omit reference to unsuccessful pregnancies, caused underestimation of the rate of total abortions for social background types 1, 2, and 3 relative to types 4, 5, and 6. The second source of error, calling induced abortions spontaneous, caused an overestimation of spontaneous abortions and an underestimation of induced abortions for social background types 4 and 6. The third source of error, calling a spontaneous abortion induced, may have caused underestimation of spontaneous abortions and overestimation of induced abortions for type 5.

We guess that the net effect was to underestimate the spontaneous abortions for types 1, 2, 3, and possibly 5 and to overestimate the spontaneous abortions for types 4 and 6. With respect to induced abortions, the rates for types 4 and 6 probably are underestimates, while the rate for type 5 is possibly an overestimate.

2. Fecundity of Social Background Types

   a. Introduction

"The physiological capacity of bearing a child to term is called fecundity."[3] Fecundity can be viewed as requiring two capacities; the capacity to conceive and the capacity to bring the resulting pregnancy to term. Both of these should be viewed as matters of degree, as should the resulting fecundity.

The purpose of this technical note is to demonstrate that the social background types studied in Chapters V, VI, and VII did not differ appreciably in fecundity.

---

[3] United Nations, Department of Social Affairs, Population Division, Multilingual Demographic Dictionary, Provisory Edition (June, 1954), New York.

b. Capacity to Conceive

A couple's average monthly chance of conception during full exposure has been called its _fecundability._ We are able to measure this only indirectly.[4]

Let us assume that the relative fecundability of a couple during the period immediately following their marriage is representative of their relative fecundability throughout their marriage. Let us further assume that the full exposure time that a couple takes to conceive after marriage is related to its monthly chance of conception, or fecundability, during that period. Then couples who, though fully exposed, did not conceive during the first five years after marriage were probably very low in average fecundability.

We can operationally define as "slow conceivers" all couples who (1) did not conceive within the first five years of marriage and who, previous to first conception, (2) had never been separated from their husbands for more than three consecutive months and (3) had never used any method to avoid conception.

The proportions of women in the social background types classed "slow conceivers" were small. They ranged from 2.8 per cent to 8.3 per cent of the women in the type.

The important question, however, is how much the differential

---

[4] A rather full discussion of the problem of measuring fecundability will be found in Chapter IV of Charles F. Westoff, Robert G. Potter, Jr., Philip C. Sagi, and Eliot G. Mishler, _Family Growth in Metropolitan America_ (in publication).

proportions of slow conceivers might have contributed to the observed fertility differences among the social background types. Table D-2 presents the total fertility rates of all women in each type. It also presents for each type the total fertility rate of only those women who were not slow conceivers.

TABLE D-2

TOTAL FERTILITY RATES OF ALL WOMEN AND OF NON-SLOW-CONCEIVING WOMEN BY SOCIAL BACKGROUND TYPE

Social background type	All women		Non-slow conceiving women		
	Number of women	Total fertility rate	Number of women	Total fertility rate	Increase
Village, uneducated					
1. Moslem	184-28	7.43	173-27	7.54	0.11
2. Christian	76-19	8.16	72-17	8.67	0.51
City, uneducated					
3. Moslem	136-30	7.35	127-30	7.63	0.28
4. Christian	96-35	4.14	88-32	4.45	0.31
City, educated					
5. Moslem	49-5	5.56	47-5	5.85	0.29
6. Christian	107-16	3.44	104-16	3.52	0.08
Standard Deviation		1.77		1.84	

Elimination of the slow conceivers, of course, raises the total fertility rate of each type. But the amount of increase does not vary much from type to type.

c. Involuntary Pregnancy Wastage

The result of a pregnancy could be live birth, still birth, spontaneous abortion, or induced abortion. Involuntary pregnancy wastage would refer to all pregnancies ending in spontaneous abortion or still birth.

118

Still births are distinguished from spontaneous abortions only in that
the pregnancy lasted for seven or more months before ending unsuccessfully.

Table D-3 reports, for each social background type, the per
cent of ended pregnancies which resulted in still births and spontaneous
abortions. The per cents that ended in either of these fates ranged from
10.4 per cent to 16.2 per cent. Furthermore, we have reason to suspect
that the per cents in the upper end of the range — those representing
uneducated and educated city Christians — are relative overestimates.[5]

TABLE D-3

PER CENT OF ENDED PREGNANCIES RESULTING IN STILL BIRTHS
AND SPONTANEOUS ABORTIONS, BY SOCIAL BACKGROUND TYPE

Social background type	Number of pregnancies ended	Spontaneous abortions	Still births	Spontaneous abortions and still births
Village, uneducated				
1. Moslems	1168	10.4%	2.3%	12,8%
2. Christians	512	10.0	2.3	12.3
City, uneducated				
3. Moslems	876	11.1	1.5	12.6
4. Christians	479	14.8	1.2	16.1
City, educated				
5. Moslems	270	7.4	3.0	10.4
6. Christians	413	13.8	2.4	16.2

d. Combined Effect of Both Factors on Fecundity

We have treated separately two aspects of biological capacity to

───────────────

[5] See Technical Note 1: Errors in Reported Pregnancy Wastage, above.

bring live birth, (1) the speed of conception and (2) the likelihood of the pregnancy resulting in live birth. In each case, we have found little variation among the social background types with respect to the characteristics.

It is still possible, however, that the combined effects of the two factors would be enough to cause concern. This would occur to the extent that the same social background types fell on the upper or the lower extremes of both factors.

If this cumulative effect did occur, we would be able to observe it in the list below. For each social background type are presented (1) its rank in terms of the negative effect that slow conceivers had on it total fertility rate and (2) its rank in terms of the rate of spontaneous abortions and still births. In both cases, the ranks run from the type most affected to the type least affected.

Social background type	Degree of effect by slow conceivers	Degree of effect by involuntary pregnancy wastage
1. Village uneducated Moslem	5	3
2. Village uneducated Christian	1	5
3. City uneducated Moslem	4	4
4. City uneducated Christian	2	2
5. City educated Moslem	3	6
6. City educated Christian	6	1

There is no evidence that these two factors combined to raise or lower the fecundity of any particular type relative to other types. In fact, the rank correlation (rho) between the factors was -.54. The two factors appear to have counterbalanced each other rather than to have supplemented each other.

We conclude that differential fecundity of social background types was not a major determinant of fertility differences among the social background types.

3. Frequency of Intercourse as a Fertility Determinant

a. Introduction

In our interviews we asked each woman "About how many times per month did you and your husband have intercourse?" We asked the question twice, once referring to the first year the woman was married and living with her husband and again referring to the period after the woman had recovered from her first live birth and before she became pregnant the next time (if, indeed, she had had any live birth). The responses are to be used with caution.[6]

b. Nature of the Effect

Our first question is how frequency of intercourse can affect speed of conception. Ryder expresses the current view, and skepticism about it:[7]

---

[6] These two questions were the most sensitive in the interview. Of the women in the social background types, 5 per cent refused to answer the question referring to the period immediately following marriage. Of the women asked the second question, 2 per cent refused to answer. Offhand responses are quite possible. On the one hand, the responses have some plausibility in that they (1) show a wide variation among women rather than clustering around some popular norm and (2) show the expected decrease in frequency of intercourse over time within marriage. On the other hand, about one-sixth of the women reported frequencies of more than 30 times a month during the first year of marriage.

[7] Ryder, op. cit., p. 417. Lorimer expresses a very similar view; op. cit., page 23.

"...it is...likely that this is a meaningful variable for the probability of conception and perhaps also for the probability of fetal mortality. Clearly, a very low coital frequency is prejudicial to the conception rate, and probably a very high frequency is too because the quantity and quality of the ejaculation is lowered. However, evidence is very weak concerning both the physiological nexus and the statistical background."

The rationale for this supposed curvilinear relationship assumes that with increased frequency of intercourse, at least at extreme frequencies, the quantity and quality of male ejaculation tends to wane. Potter's recent summary of medical literature on this subject casts doubt on this assumption.[8]

---

[8] Robert G. Potter, Jr. "Length of the Fertile Period" (forthcoming in the Milbank Memorial Fund Quarterly). Potter's summary of the literature on which this conclusion is based is worth quoting: "In a series of articles published in Fertility and Sterility, J. MacLeod and R. Z. Gold have shown, in a convincing way, that sperm count in a secondary factor except when it falls below a minimum, estimated to be in the neighborhood of 20 million sperms per c. c. or 60 million total. Given a sperm count above this minimum, the important factors for virility — among those few factors measurable in large samples — become the percentage of active sperms and the character of their movement. Heightened coital frequency does not appear to penalize either quality. Furthermore, coital frequencies of 3 or 4 times per week do not depress the sperm counts of most males below, or even near, critical levels. Of special relevance, among several pertinent articles, is "The Male Factor in Fertility and Infertility: Semen Quality in Relation to Age and Sexual Activity," Fertility and Sterility, January-February, 1953, 4, 10-23. For the oligospermatic male who barely meets, or fails to meet, the minimum sperm count even after several days of continence, increase from moderate to high coital frequencies may lower conception chances. Cf. Farris, Edmund J.: Human Fertility and Problems of the Male, pp. 101-119. The incidence of oligospermatic males in the general population is not known. MacLeod and Gold find that 7 per cent of the husbands from 936 fertile unions have total sperm counts below 50 million while the corresponding frequency among husbands from 783 infertile unions is 15 per cent: "Spermatozoon Counts in 1,000 Men of Known Fertility and 1,000 Cases of Infertile Marriages." Journal of Urology, 1951, 66, p. 439."

> "...the results of MacLeod and Gold suggest that male
> virility is not ordinarily jeopardized by increased
> sexual activity except possibly when the male is
> oligospermatic or when the increase is to very high
> coital frequencies..."

If the factor of male virility is indeed negligible, then one would expect

any relationship between coital frequency and speed of conception to be

linear, save for the effect of yet another factor: Potter notes that, "as

coital frequency increases, so does the chance of 2 or more coitions

coinciding with the same fertile period, with all but the first of this set

of coitions rendered in some degree superfluous."[9]

To summarize, relationships of three kinds have been suggested

between coital frequency and speed of conception: (1) The relationship

is positive up to a point, then becomes negative. (2) The relationship

is positive throughout. (3) The relationship is positive up to extreme

coital frequency, where the relationship tends to disappear.

Three studies of this topic on clinical populations in the United

States do not show the first type of relationship; the curvilinear one.

Among MacLeod and Gold's sample of "fertile" couples using the clinic

in a New York hospital, as reported coital frequency increased from 2

times per week to 4 or more times per week, the proportion of couples

conceiving in 5 months or less rose systematically from .29 to .46 to

.52 to .83.[10] Stix asked her clinical population (of Cincinnati white

women who did not practice contraception before their first pregnancy)

---

[9] Ibid.

[10] J. MacLeod and R. Z. Gold, "The Male Factor in Fertility and Infertility: Semen Quality and Certain Other Factors in Relation to Ease of Conception," Fertility and Sterility, January-February, 1953, 4, Table 19, p. 29.

123

the number of months between marriage and first pregnancy. As coital frequency increased from 2 times per week to 5 or more times per week, the mean conception delay decreased from 8.4 months to 6.9 months to 5.2 months to 4.5 months.[11] Stix and Notestein, using a similar method on a New York clinical population, found a relationship similar in nature, but of doubtful significance.[12] At least two of these studies agree in showing a linear relationship, and give no evidence of a decline in this relationship at extreme coital frequencies.

Our data permit us to replicate these studies on a sample which is neither clinical nor American. We have used a method very similar to that used by Stix and by Stix and Notestein, cited above. For each frequency of intercourse subclass, we computed the mean months between marriage and first conception.[13] The results are presented in Table D-4.

---

[11] R. K. Stix, "Birth Control in a Mid-Western City; I." Milbank Memorial Fund Quarterly, January, 1939, 17, Table 6, p. 82. It is to be noted that speed of conception is an indirect measure of the probability of conception in any given months or series of months.

[12] R. K. Stix and F. W. Notestein, Controlled Fertility. Baltimore: Williams and Wilkins Co., 1940, Table 11, p. 34.

[13] Women married before 1920 were excluded. Also excluded were all women so slow in conceiving that they could be suspected of total infecundability; that is, all women who had not conceived during the first five years of marriage although using no method to avoid conception. Also excluded were women who used any method to delay the first pregnancy or who were separated from their husbands for more than three consecutive months before the first conception. Since the age of the woman at marriage probably affected her speed of first conception, we eliminated women married at extremely early or extremely late ages and classified the remaining women into two categories on the basis of age at marriage.

TABLE D-4

MEAN MONTHS BETWEEN MARRIAGE AND FIRST CONCEPTION BY FREQUENCY OF INTERCOURSE DURING FIRST YEAR OF MARRIAGE AND AGE OF WOMAN AT MARRIAGE

| Coital frequency per month during first year of marriage | Age of woman at marriage | | | |
| | 14 to 17 | | 18 to 27 | |
	Number of women	Mean months	Number of women	Mean months
0 to 10	41	8.2	57	6.1
11 to 20	87	7.5	125	5.6
21 to 30	103	7.1	110	5.4
more than 30	64	5.5	51	3.1
Total	295*		343**	

*Does not include 14 refusals.
**Does not include 20 refusals.

The correlations represented by this table are quite small. The Pearsonian coefficients between coital frequency and months to first conception were .06 for women married at ages 14 to 17 and .09 for women married at ages 18 to 27.

Moreover, even these small coefficients are questionable. Most of the association rests on the considerably lower mean months to first conception of women reporting coital frequencies of more than 30 per month during the first year of marriage. That this high a frequency for the first year of marriage was true of the proportion of women reporting it seems incredible.[14] Nor does our review of the literature describe the physiological mechanism by which coital frequency in this upper part of the range could affect speed of conception.

There is little evidence that this small relationship is curvilinear in nature. Within each age-at-marriage class, the mean months to first conception drops systematically as frequency of intercourse during the first year after marriage increases. Furthermore, the curvilinear correlation coefficients between the two characteristics are only slightly larger than the linear correlation coefficients.[15] To the degree that there is any curve suggested by the means, it is not the curve suggested by Ryder.

---

[14] One might argue that some linear correlation would be automatic from our method of analysis. Frequency of intercourse within the first year of marriage may decrease markedly from the "honeymoon" period. The woman conceiving early might characterize her first year of intercourse by this high early frequency; the woman conceiving later is more likely to remember the decreased frequency later in the year. The extremely high frequencies reported by women averaging short periods to first conception seem to support this interpretation.

[15] Comparison between E coefficients and r coefficients of correlation for the same data furnish an estimate of how far the relationship differs from linearity in nature. For the women married at ages 14 to 17, the E was .10 and the r was .06; for the women married at ages 18 to 27, the E was .12 and the r was .09. The class intervals of frequency of intercourse used in computing the above E coefficients are those presented in Table D-4.

c. Differences among Social Background Types

Supposing that frequency of intercourse does have some slight positive effect on fertility, the next question is whether or not coital frequency differs for the six social background types under study. Table D-5 presents the median coital frequency per month for each social background type.[16]

The expected *time* patterns appear. In each social background type, the median frequency during the first year after marriage was higher than between the first live birth and the next conception. One could expect a continued decrease in frequency over time in marriage. This would result in more similarity between the frequencies of classes later in the marriage, as all classes approach very low frequencies.

The coital frequency differences among the types at these early stages of marriage are small and indeed complex. Moslems tended to have higher frequency than Christians, but not among the uneducated city dwellers. Moslem uneducated villagers tended to have higher frequency than Moslem uneducated city dwellers, but this was not true of the Christians. Educated city Moslems seem to have had higher frequencies than uneducated city Moslems, but this was not true of Christians. Moreover, the coital frequencies of the types seem to bear little relation to the total fertility rates of the types.

---

[16] See Appendix F, Table F-36: Percentage Distribution of Coital Frequency by Social Background Type for Two Time Periods.

TABLE D-5

MEDIAN FREQUENCY OF INTERCOURSE PER MONTH BY
SOCIAL BACKGROUND TYPE

Social background type	Frequency during first year of marriage		Frequency between first live birth and next pregnancy		Total fertility rate of type***
	Number of women	Median	Number of women	Median	
Village, uneducated					
1. Moslem	165	24.5	164	18.6	7.43
2. Christian	70	18.2	69	11.7	8.16
City, uneducated					
3. Moslem	134	19.1	131	12.9	7.35
4. Christian	92	19.8	87	12.3	4.14
City, educated					
5. Moslem	48	21.2	47	17.1	5.56
6. Christian	106	17.9	104	13.1	3.44
TOTAL	615*		602**		

*Does not include 33 women who refused to answer the question on frequency of intercourse during the first year, 19 of them from social background type 1.

**Does not include 11 women who refused to answer the question on frequency of intercourse during this period, 6 of them from social background type 1. Also excludes women who never had a live birth.

***Based on all 648 women falling into social background types.

d. As an Explanation of Fertility Differences

In sum, we have little reason to believe that differential frequency of intercourse contributed much to the fertility differences among the social background types. The relationship between coital frequency and speed of conception was slight and questionable. The social background types did not show extreme differences in average

128

coital frequency even early in marriage, and the differences seemed
to be decreasing as marriage progressed. The coital frequency
differences that did exist did not relate to the total fertility differences
among the social background types.

4. Correcting for Induced Abortion

Each total fertility rate is the sum of the five specific fertility
rates for five successive periods of marriage.[17] Each specific fertility rate has as its numerator the number of live births occurring in
a five-year period of marriage to women completing that period. Its
denominator is the number of women completing the period. The denominator also can be viewed as the number of woman months taken
to produce these live births, divided by 60 (the number of months in
five years).

The method of correcting for induced abortions was to eliminate
from the denominators of specific fertility rates estimates of the total
woman months wasted by inducing abortions. The best estimate of the
months wasted by inducing a given abortion seemed the number of
months between the conception ending in the induced abortion and the
next conception experienced by the woman. If the conception ending in
the induced abortion was not followed by another conception by the
woman, the months wasted were assumed to have been fourteen; this
arbitrary number had been observed to be a rough average of months
wasted per induced abortion by women who did have a succeeding con-

---

[17] For the method of computing total fertility rates see Chapter III,
pp.____.

ception.[18/] The estimated months wasted by induced abortions for a class of women and for a given period of marriage would be the total months wasted during that period of marriage by women in the class who completed that period.

The procedure for correcting any specific fertility rate is described below:

Let s_c = the corrected specific fertility rate.

n = the number of women in the class completing the period of marriage.

c = the number of woman-months wasted by those n women by induced abortions occurring during that period of marriage.

b = the number of live births by those n women during that period of marriage.

Then $s_c = \dfrac{b}{n = \dfrac{c}{60}}$

The corrected total fertility rate for any class of women was obtained by adding the five corrected specific fertility rates for the five periods of marriage.

[18/] It should be noted that we are not taking into account the effect of permanent sterility caused by induced abortion in our correction of fertility rates. The use of a 14-month constant as an estimate of the months wasted by induced abortions not followed by other conceptions is admittedly the weakest part of the estimation procedure. It was necessary to apply this constant to eighteen per cent of the induced abortions counted in Table VI-2, Chapter VI.

INTERVIEW SCHEDULE AND INSTRUCTIONS[1]

1. Introducing the Interview

When you start talking with the potential respondent, the first things to do are (1) to establish rapport, (2) to make sure that she should be a respondent, and (3) to arrange for the best interviewing situation.

Establishing Rapport

Establishing rapport is best accomplished by (a) immediately identifying yourself and justifying your presence and (b) convincing the woman of the importance of her cooperation.

(a) The easiest way to identify yourself is to show the woman your identification card from the Ministry of Social Affairs (or mentioning some local leader who has prepared the woman for your visit, if this is the case).

(b) Getting the woman's cooperation may be best accomplished by stating the content of the following statement at this point:

"A group of doctors have decided that they need to know more about Lebanese couples and their children. They need to know how many children Lebanese couples have, and what problems couples meet in taking care of these children. They need this information to give better advice when couples ask for it.

"These doctors believe that only Lebanese wives can tell them what they need to know. So they have sent me, and several other Lebanese women, to ask some questions.

"This has nothing to do with the government, although the Ministry of Social Affairs has tried to help the doctors in gathering the facts.

---

1. Detailed interviewer instructions were mimeographed separately from the interview schedule, and carried separately by each interviewer. In this presentation, instructions are presented immediately after the interview schedule questions to which they refer.

"The doctors do not want the names of the women. No
one, not even the doctors, will know who gave what facts.

If the woman asks "what doctors," show the sponsorship
cards you think appropriate for that particular woman. Read
off the names if it appears that the woman cannot read.

a. Establishing if the Woman Should be Interviewed

The next step is to determine if the woman you are
talking to should be a respondent, and if there are any other
respondents living in that dwelling unit. This may be accomplished by asking the following questions immediately after
you have finished the above introductory statement:

"First, let me find if you are one of the women that
the doctors need to know more about.

    (a) "Have you yourself ever been married for five years
        or more?"

    (b) "Have you been married more than once?"

    (c) "Are you a Lebanese citizen; that is, do you own
        a Lebanese identity card?"

Ask only enough of these questions to determine if the
woman should be interviewed. She should be interviewed only if
(a) she has been married for more than five years, (b) has been
married only once and (c) is a Lebanese citizen.

If the woman should not be a respondent, first find out
about any other potential respondents in the dwelling unit.
Do this by asking her if there are any other women in this
house who have the qualifications. Ask to talk to them if
they are there. If they are not there, ask when you might be
able to speak to them. Finally, excuse yourself, being sure
to thank her for her time; it is extremely important that you
make a good impression on this woman, since she will tell of
her experience to other potential respondents.

b. Establishing the Best Interview Situation

If the woman should be a respondent, immediately try
to get her cooperation. The content of the following statement should help:

"Then you are one of the wives the doctors want me to
question. What you tell me about your family will be put
together with information from many other wives. They do not
want your name. Nobody will ever know which wife gave what
facts. You need not tell me anything you do not choose to
tell me."

Answer any questions the woman has about the study and about what will be asked of her. Take enough time to allay any fears she might have. Make sure that you do not lead her to believe that she will be directly rewarded for her cooperation in some material way.

Then try to set up the best interviewing situation, a situation where you can talk with the woman alone for a period of one half hour or more in a place where you can write. If this requires setting up an appointment for some other time, by all means do so. Future appointments are likely to be necessary when the woman is very busy, when the woman has guests, or when the woman is on her way out. Caution: if you feel that the woman is asking for a future appointment as a method for completely avoiding the interview, work a little more on gaining rapport until you get a firm commitment to an appointment or a definite refusal.

When you bring out your interview schedule, say something like the following: "The doctors want me to write down exactly what you say, so they can be sure that they are getting exactly the truth."

In order to set up an efficient procedure with the woman, say something like the following: "As you can see, there are many questions, I have found that we can complete this best if you will let me ask them in order, and you answer them one by one. Can we do that?"

2. General Instructions

The interview schedule has been revised considerably on the basis of the pretest results. We believe that it should be much easier for you to use now.

In the pretest, you were urged to record all information necessary for us to know to revise the questions. The emphasis is now changed; it is on completeness and reliability.

By completeness is meant the recording of all of the information requested about each woman interviewed. Every appropriate question must be asked, and an answer recorded or the whole interview is worthless to the study (and the interviewer will not be paid for the interview). The only legitimate reasons for lack of recorded information is a genuine refusal by the woman or genuine lack of knowledge by the woman, even after the interviewer has done her best to get a response; such responses should be indicated by "refusal" or "don't know" in the appropriate spaces. A blank space where a response is needed for that woman will result in nonpayment for the interview.

Completeness also means getting the full responses of
the woman by patient probing. For instance, this means probing to get all of the methods for delaying pregnancy that the
woman has heard about, in response to question 31.

By reliability is meant, not only truthfulness, but also
the likelihood that some other interviewer would get exactly
the same responses from the same woman. As a guide, ask yourself "If another good interviewer were performing this interview, would she be getting exactly the same answers as I am?"
If you can answer "yes" to this question, you are getting reliable responses. Obviously, being reliable eliminates the
possibility of putting words into the woman's mouth or making
mild guesses about what the woman really means from an inartic-
ulate statement. You must probe for the woman's real history
and opinions before you can get reliable answers.

From time to time we will check to see how reliable
are the responses being obtained by interviewers. We will do
this by sending another interviewer around to reinterview
the same woman again on some of the questions, then compare
these answers with the answers that you get.

In order to make this possible, it is essential that
you give a full description of how this woman can be located
for reinterview in answer to question 50 of the interview
schedule. This should be filled out after you have completed
the interview, but before you have a chance to forget the
details of location. Any interview schedule without this
detailed information is an incomplete interview schedule, and
will not be paid for.

Wording of Questions

Many interviewers found the specific colloquial wording
of questions in the pretest interview schedule was difficult
to use. For this reason, we have adopted the following policy
on question wording:

Questions referring to specific facts are in the form
of classical Arabic statements describing exactly the fact
requested. The interviewer must find exactly the fact described,
but may use her own words in asking and probing for the fact.
(Even factual questions, however, must be asked in the order
they are presented on the interview schedule; interviewers do
not have the liberty to reorder questions as they choose.)

Questions referring to opinions or feelings are written
in question form and in colloquial Arabic, with quotation
marks. These questions must be asked verbatim, since different

words are known to bring different responses. Even when probing on these questions, use the words given in the question
or the words suggested for probing, exactly.

Ordering of Questions

The order in which the questions appear is the order in
which they should be asked. Do not change the order to suit
the whim of the respondent. A question changed in place is
not the same question to the respondent, especially when it
comes to matters of opinion.

As in the pretest, not every woman will be asked every
question. We have tried to simplify your job by putting beside
each response category to the previous question which question
should be asked next. In all cases where no such directions
are given, then the question with the next number is to be
asked next. In all cases where the next numbered question is
to be omitted, you will find directions about what question
to ask next for woman. Make sure that you follow these instructions exactly. If you do not, you will end up either
alienating the respondent or with an incomplete and worthless
interview.

Types of responses

The interview schedule is constructed so that you will
never have to write a word, except on the last page or when
you are uncertain of a classification. Under ideal conditions,
the woman's responses all can be recorded either as a simple
number or as a check.

Sometimes we ask for years of age of persons. This always means the years completed by the specified date, not rounded
to the nearest year.

On the other hand, we frequently ask for the months
during which something occurred or the months between events.
Here we want you to round off to the nearest month; for instance, the months that a woman nursed a child would be eleven
months if she actually nursed him 10 months and 20 days.

Several questions ask you to classify the woman's response in terms of the classes described at the bottom of the
page. The procedure is to get the woman to give a full response to the question in her own words (for instance, her
husband's occupation), then choose the category best summarizing the statement the woman has made. Only if her response
is not described by any of the classes given do you need to
write out her response.

135

<u>Interviewer</u> <u>Comments</u>

Spaces for interviewer comments are given at the bottom of each page. The interviewer should record anything which might help us to interpret recorded responses to questions. However, she should not use these spaces <u>instead</u> <u>of</u> the response categories for questions.

3. <u>Interview</u> <u>Schedule</u> <u>and</u> <u>Specific</u> <u>Instructions</u>

"Let me start by asking a few questions about your marriage and your family."
----

1. a. Is the woman married <u>now</u>?

_____yes (proceed to question 2)

_____no

b. In what year did her marriage end? _____
                                        (year)

[The woman is not married now if, at the time of the interview, she was a widow, or had been divorced, or considered herself no longer married to her first husband. If the marriage ended by one of these three methods, we need the year in which the death, divorce, or separation took place.]

2. How many years of age was the woman at the time of her marriage?
                                        (years)

3. How many years of age was the woman's husband at the time he married the woman?
                                        (years)

[In both questions 2 and 3, "years of age" refers to the <u>years</u> <u>completed</u> at the time of the interview. Thus a woman born 25 years and 11 months before the interview would be 25 years of age.]

4. How many brothers and how many sisters did the woman
   have who were living at the time she was married?

   number of brothers   _____

   number of sisters   _____

   [We are after the size of the family the woman considered her own at the time she was married. If she asks
   about whether to include certain people as brother or
   sisters (for instance, half brothers) ask her to include
   them if she considered them brothers or sisters at that
   time.]

5. a. Has the woman born any sons or daughters who are now
      living?

      _____yes

      _____no (proceed to question 6)

   b. How many of these children are now living?

      (number)

   c. How many years of age is her eldest living
      child now? (either boy or girl)

      (years)

   [We want to know the woman's living biological family,
   children she herself has given birth to, not including any
   adoptions, etc. In questions c, we want the years completed by the oldest of these children still living no
   matter whether that child is a boy or a girl.]

6. In what year and month did the woman marry?
   (probe and estimate)   year _____

   number of month _____

   [This is the only date that we will ask in the whole
   interview schedule; all other dates will be figured by
   reference to this one. Therefore, it is essential that
   you probe until you have established this date exactly.
   One way to establish the date is as follows: Use the
   information about the age of her oldest living child and
   ask her how long after her marriage this child was born,
   then substract the total of these two periods from the
   present date. The numbering of months starts with January
   as the first month and December as the twelfth.]

137

"Doctors believe that knowing a couple's history before they
were married helps to understand their family problems after
they were married. I would like to ask you some questions
about you and your husband during the five years before you
two were married."
----

7. a. In what community did the woman live most of the five
       years before her marriage? (probe)

       Was that community a city, or was it a town or village
       during those years? (probe and classify) (check one)

       _____ city

       _____ town or village

       _____ not sure of class,
              Name of community _____

              Nation of the community now _____

              Total population then _____

              Per cent of men farmers then _____

              Other information _____

              _____

    b. During those years when the woman was living in (above
       community), did the woman usually move to some other
       community for more than one month of each year?

       _____ yes

       _____ no (proceed to question 8)

    c. Was that community a city, or was it a town or village
       during those years?

       _____ city

       _____ town or village

       _____ not sure of class,
              Name of community _____
              Nation of the community now _____
              Total population then _____
              Per cent of men farmers then _____
              Other information _____
              _____
                     138

[The purpose of questions 7 and 8 is to determine whether the woman and her husband had rural or urban backgrounds, or combinations of these, during the last five years before their marriage. The first step is to determine in what community the person lived most of the five years before marriage, that is, the community in which he or she was eating and sleeping for the largest part of the five years. The name of this community need not be written, unless the interviewer is not sure whether it was a city or a town or village during these five years previous to the marriage.

A city is a community with a population of more than 20,000 people and with more than half of its men working in non-farming jobs. In Lebanon, only Beirut and Tripoli are to be considered cities; all other Lebanese communities are to be considered towns or villages.

If the interviewer is not sure whether the community is a city or not, she should write the name, nation, and as much as possible of the requested information about the community in the spaces provided under "not sure of class."

Question b is to determine whether or not the person while he or she was living in the above home community before marriage usually went to some other community for part of each year. We are referring to habitual, patterned behavior here, such as the migration of wealthy Lebanese from Beirut to the mountain villages during the summer months. If the person did usually move to some other community, find out the kind of community this was in the same manner as you did for the home community.[1]]

8. a. In what community did her husband live most of the five years before he married the woman? (probe)

    Was that community a city, or was it a town or village during those years? (probe and classify) (check one)

    _____ city

    _____ town or village

    _____ not sure of class. Name of community _____

        Nation of the community now _____

        Total population then _____

        Per cent men farmers then _____

        Other information _____

        _____

---

1. In editing, visitation to Europe was assumed to mean visitation to a city.

b. During those years when the husband was living in (above community) did the husband usually move to some other community for <u>more</u> <u>than</u> <u>one</u> <u>month</u> of each year?

_____ yes

_____ no (proceed to question 9)

c. Was that community a city, or was it a town or village during <u>those</u> <u>years</u>?

_____ city

_____ town or village

_____ not sure of class.
Name of community _____

Nation of the community <u>now</u> _____

Total population <u>then</u> _____

Per cent of men farmers <u>then</u> _____

Other information _____

_____

_____

_____

9. a. Did the husband ever receive elementary certificate or higher educational degree?

    _____ yes (ask question b only)

    _____ no (ask question c only)

    b. What was the <u>highest</u> degree the husband received?

    _____ elementary certificate

    _____ Lebanese Brivet

    _____ some degree higher than a Lebanese Brivet

    _____ not sure of classification of degree. (describe degree below)

    name of degree _____

    school or educational system _____

    minimum total years of
    schooling required for degree _____

    c. Can the husband read and write more than his own name?

    _____ yes

    _____ no

    [Questions 9 and 10: Since the woman is more likely to remember the degrees that she and her husband have obtained than the years of schooling, we are asking the interviewer to probe for the degrees. Unless the person has some higher degree, be sure to probe to find whether she or he has an elementary certificate. By obtaining a degree, we do not mean attending school for a certain number of years, but actually passing the examinations for that degree. Below are the kinds of degrees falling into each of the classes:

    Lebanese (or other) elementary certificate. This degree usually requires a minimum of five years of schooling or the equivalent.

    Lebanese Brivet or 1st secondary degree. This usually involves at least four years of schooling beyond the elementary degree.

141

Some degree higher than the Lebanese Brivet. This should include Baccalaureates 1 and 2, all college degrees any U. S. high school degree or, in general, any degree which required more than nine years of formal schooling or which was obtained after the Lebanese Brivet.

In all cases check the class representing the last degree obtained. For instance, a person who studied four years after his or her Lebanese Brivet, but received no further degree for this work, would still be classified as "Lebanese Brivet." If you are not sure of how to classify the last degree obtained, get the requested information from the woman, and write it in the space provided.

If the person has never received an elementary certificate, we want to know whether or not he or she can read and write more than their own name. The interviewer must probe for this, evaluate the truthfulness of the woman's response, and record the interviewer's best guess as an answer.]

10. a. Did the woman ever receive an elementary certificate or any higher educational degree?

_____ yes (ask question b only)

_____ no (ask question c only)

b. What was the highest degree the woman received?

_____ elementary certificate

_____ Lebanese Brivet

_____ Some degree higher than the Lebanese Brivet.

_____ Not sure of classification of degree. (describe degree below)

name of degree _____

School or educational system _____

minimum total years of
schooling required for degree _____

c. Can the woman read and write more than her own name?
(prob
_____ yes

_____ no

142

11. a. During the last five years before she was married, did
       the woman ever work _for money_?

       ____ yes

       ____ no (proceed to question 12)

    b. Ask about the best-paying position she had during these
       years. In this position, did the woman work _most of the
       time_ at home or away from home?

       ____ at home

       ____ away from home

    c. Ask about this best-paying position.

       "If you had not married, do you believe that you could
       have supported yourself by staying in that position?"

       ____ yes

       ____ no

12. To what religious sect did the woman belong immediately
    after her marriage?

             number of class _____

             other sect (name) _____

        [In questions 12 and 13, we want the sect to which
    each partner belonged during the period right after marriage.
    This may or may not be the sects to which they belong at
    the time of the interview or belonged before marriage.
    Record the sect by putting the number of the appropriate
    class of sects in the indicated space. If (and only if)
    the sect does not fall into any of these classes, write the
    name of the sect   in the space beside "other sect."

143

13. To what religious sect did the woman's husband belong immediately after his marriage to the woman?

        number of class _____

        other sect (name) _____

Religious Sect Classes

1. Sunnite Moslem
2. Shiite Moslem
3. Druze
4. Maronite Catholic
5. Catholic not Maronite, such as Roman or Latin Catholic, Greek Catholic, Armenian Catholic, Syrian Catholic, etc.
6. Greek Orthodox, Russian Orthodox
7. Orthodox not Greek, such as Armenian Orthodox, Syrian Orthodox, etc.
8. Protestant Christian
9. No religious identification.

144

"Now let me ask a few questions about you and your husband
 during the first five years after you were married."

14. a. In what community did the woman live most of the first
        five years <u>after</u> her marriage?

        Was that community a city, or was it a town or village
        <u>during those years</u>? (probe and classify) (check one)

        ____ city

        ____ town or village

        ____ not sure of class.
             Name of community _____

                Nation of the community <u>now</u> _____

                Total population <u>then</u> _____

                Per cent of men farmers <u>then</u> _____

                Other information _____

                _____

     b. During those years when the woman was living in (above
        community), did the woman <u>usually</u> move to some other
        community for <u>more than one month</u> of each year?

        ____ yes

        ____ no (proceed to question 15)

     c. Was that community a city, or was it a town or village
        <u>during those years</u>?

        ____ city

        ____ town or village

        ____ not sure of class.
             Name of community _____

                Nation of the community <u>now</u> _____

                Total population <u>then</u> _____

                Per cent of men farmers <u>then</u> _____

                Other information _____

                _____

        [For question 14, use the same instructions as for
     questions 7 and 8.]

145

15. (Remind the woman of the name of the community which she said was her home most of the first five years after she married. All of the following questions refer to that part of the first five years after her marriage when she had this community as her home.)

a. Did her husband earn most of his yearly income by himself farming (working on the land), or did he earn most of his yearly income in some other way?

_____ most by himself farming (ask question b only)

_____ most in some other way (ask question c only)

_____ don't know (proceed to question 16)

b. Was any of the land the husband farmed either owned by the husband or lent to the husband by relatives?

_____ yes (proceed to question 16)

_____ no (proceed to question 16)

_____ don't know (proceed to question 16)

c. From what type of activity did her husband earn most of his yearly income during those years?

number of class _____

not sure of class (describe occupation).

_____

_____

_____

_____

Non-Farming Occupation Classes

1. **Profession**, for which a specific educational degree is usually required. Examples: doctor, dentist, pharmacist, lawyer, teacher in secondary school or college, etc.

2. **Commerce or industry.** Examples: owner or operator of industry of commercial establishment making income off the sale of goods, renter of urban or rural property earning income either in money or crops, investor in enterprises drawing profits from investments, agent for commercial or insurance establishment working on a commission basis, etc.

3. **Clerical**, occupations in which he is paid primarily for skills in reading, writing, bookkeeping, filing, etc. Examples: government clerk, stenographer, secretary, etc.

4. **Skilled work or craft**, usually earning more than LL. 200 per month. Salaried workers for organizations whose positions involve use of unusual skills, such as railroad telephone lineman, teacher of driving, machinist in factory, etc. Also self-employed craftsmen who make money from some particular skill, such as jewelers, blacksmiths, etc.

5. **Unskilled worker or servant**, usually earning less than LL200 per month. Examples: daily laborers, night guards, clerks in stores, taxi drivers or chauffers, waiters, etc.

6. **Unemployed**, gaining most of income from sources other than own work.

[Question 15 refers to the period of time when the family had the residential pattern described in question 14. Question a is to determine whether the husband was primarily a farmer or a non-farmer. Question b is to classify the farmers on the basis of land ownership.

Question c is to classify primarily non-farmers on the basis of their basic type of occupation. The interviewer should ask the woman how her husband earned his income during those years, which might be several ways. She should then ask which way he earned most of his income. After getting a full description of the main sources of income, the interviewer should put the number of the class best describing the activities which were the main source of income. Only in the case that the interviewer cannot decide on the most appropriate class should she describe the occupation in words, but then she should describe it in detail.]

16. (Establish the dwelling unit in which she ate most of her
     meals when she was living in her home community (14a)
     during the first five years of marriage.)

     a. At the time she first moved to that dwelling unit, how
         many rooms were there in the dwelling unit, not including
         storage rooms? (probe)

                                                        _____
                                                         (number)

     b. How many people usually slept in that dwelling
         unit? (probe)
                                                        _____
                                                         (number)

              Number of these people then less than
              10 years old?   _____

              Number of these people then between
              10 and 20 years old?   _____

              Number of these people then more than
              20 years old?   _____

         [In questions 16 and 17, a dwelling unit is any room
or set of rooms which has a separate entrance to the outside,
or onto a hallway which enters onto the outside. Count all
rooms used for living, including kitchens, bathroom, etc.
The only rooms which should not be counted are those used
only for storage, such as closets. Be careful; even though
the woman may still be living in the same dwelling unit as
she did right after marriage, the number of rooms may have
been changed.

         The people who usually slept in that dwelling unit are
those who slept there most of the nights of the year. Accept the woman's guesses about the ages of the people sleeping there, but be sure that you have made clear about the
specific time you are speaking about.]

17. (Establish the dwelling unit in which the woman now eats
     most of her meals.)

     a. How many rooms are there in that dwelling unit, not
         including storage rooms? (probe)
                                                        _____
                                                         (number)
     b. How many people usually sleep in that dwelling
         unit? (probe)
                                                        _____
                                                         (number)

              Number of these people less than 10
              years old?   _____

              Number of these people between 10 and
              20 years old?   _____

              Number of these people more than 20
              years old?   _____

"You have been very patient in answering these questions about your background. Now we come to the questions which the doctors consider the most important to them. I hope that you will give them very frank and honest answers."

		Pregnancy Number								
		1	2	3	4	5	6	7	8	9
18.	a. Months between marriage and end of 1st pregnancy. (number)									
	b. Months between end of last pregnancy and end of this pregnancy. (number)									
19.	Months pregnancy lasted									
20.	Result of pregnancy (check)									
	live birth (question 22)									
	still birth (next pregnancy)									
	abortion (question 21)									
21.	Cause of abortion (check)									
	induced (next pregnancy)									
	spontaneous (next pregnancy)									
22.	Children born (numbers)									
	males (question 23)									
	females (question 23)									
23.	(All) children still living?									
	yes (question 25)									
	no (question 24)									
24.	Years of age at death									
	male (question 25)									
	female (question 25)									
25.	Months nursed by the woman (next pregnancy)									
26.	(Interviewer leave blank.) Months not pregnant before									

149

	10	11	12	13	14	15	16	17	18
18. b. Months between end of last pregnancy and end of this pregnancy. (number)									
19. Months pregnancy lasted									
20. Result of pregnancy (check)									
live birth (question 22)									
still birth (next pregnancy)									
abortion (question 21)									
21. Cause of abortion (check)									
induced (next pregnancy)									
spontaneous (next pregnancy)									
22. Children born (numbers)									
males (question 23)									
females (question 23)									
23. (All) Children still living?									
yes (question 25)									
no (question 24)									
24. Years of age at death									
male (question 25)									
female (question 25)									
25. Months nursed by woman (next pregnancy)									
26. (Interviewer leave blank.) Months not pregnant before									

[Questions 18 through 25 should be answered about each pregnancy before going on to the next pregnancy. Not all questions should be answered for all pregnancies; the exact question to be asked next is indicated after each response category. In all cases, the interviewer should probe with her own words until she has obtained the exact information requested.

Question 18. Question a should only be answered for the first pregnancy. The months should be rounded to the nearest month; for instance, if a woman was married 10 months and 17 days before the end of her first pregnancy, the figure "11" should be put in the space. Question b should be asked for all later pregnancies, and the months rounded in the same way; for instance the number in column 2 would be the number of months between the end of the 1st pregnancy and the end of the second pregnancy. Please note, the pregnancy numbers are not necessarily the numbers of live births.

Question 19. It is essential that the interviewer get the woman's best guess of the number of months of pregnancy, whether or not it ended in a live birth. Do not automatically put down "9" for every live birth, since some pregnancies lasting 7 to 10 months can result in live births. Round off to the nearest month.

Question 20. This should be answered by checking one of the blanks. The pregnancy ended in "live birth" if the child's heart was beating at the time it was born, even if it died hours later. The pregnancy ended in "still birth" if the child's heart was not beating at the time of delivery, and the pregnancy had lasted seven months or more. The pregnancy ended in an "abortion" if the child's heart was not beating at the time of delivery and the number of months of pregnancy was less than seven. Thus, it is essential that you have answered question 19 accurately in order to answer question 20 accurately.

Question 21 is necessary to determine the cause of any abortions recorded in question 20. The abortion was "induced" if anyone did anything with the intention of stopping the pregnancy, no matter what they did. The abortion was spontaneous if nobody did anything with the intention of bringing the pregnancy to an end.

Question 22 is to register the number and sexes of children resulting from this live birth. It is to be answered by putting the number of children of each sex born alive in this pregnancy. Thus, a single male child would be recorded by putting the number "1" by males and leaving

151

the space by females blank. Twin girls would be recorded
by putting the number "2" by females and leaving the space
by males blank. Remember to record all children whose
hearts were beating at the time of delivery.

Question 24 is to determine the age at death of
those children born alive but who have died since, even
if it occurred weeks after birth. We want the answer
in years of life completed by time of death. For instance,
a child who died 11 months after birth would have "0" recorded in the blank, the correct blank being determined
by the sex of the child.

Question 25 refers to the number of months that the
respondent herself nursed this child, rounded off to the
nearest month. Do not let the woman give you a general
statement about how long she usually nurses her children
and apply that to all of her children; ask the question
specifically for each pregnancy.

Caution: On several of these pregnancy history
questions the woman may attempt to describe a general
pattern for her pregnancies, and ask you to record the
general pattern as applying exactly to each of her pregnancies. Do not do this. Get the specific information about
each pregnancy separately, as politely as you can but as pre-
cisely as you can. You are likely to run into trouble particularly on questions 18b, 19, and 25.]

27. a. Is the woman pregnant now?

     ____ yes

     ____ no (proceed to question 28)

b. How many months pregnant?   _____

                              (number)

[Question 27 may have been answered already by the
woman; if so, simply record the answer. If not, be sure
to ask the question and record the response.]

a. Was there any time when the woman was not pregnant, and
   when her husband was away from home for three or more
   consecutive months?   (probe)

   ____ yes (ask questions b and c)

   ____ no (proceed to question 29

b. Before what pregnancies did
   this occur?   (probe)
   (identification numbers)

c. Before this pregnancy, how
   many months was he consecutively away without visiting
   his wife?   (number of months)

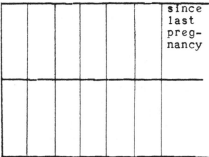

						since last pregnancy

[Both questions 28 and 29 refer to the periods when
the woman was not pregnant but was married, times when
she could have become pregnant. The questions refer to
two possible reasons for the woman not becoming pregnant
during these periods.

Question 28 refers to prolonged absence of the husband.
If the woman says that there was one or more periods of
three or more months when the husband was absent, put the
numbers of the pregnancies that these periods preceded in
the first row of the table. Use the numbers for those
pregnancies established in the pregnancy history. If the
absence has occurred since the last pregnancy listed in
the pregnancy history, make the subsequent entries under
"since last pregnancy." Question c requests that you get
the largest number of months consecutively absent by the
husband before each particular pregnancy listed for question b.

Question 29 is to be answered in the same general way:
List the pregnancy numbers in answer to question b. List
the approximate number of months of abstinence in the row
beside question c. Question d should be asked verbatim,
and a check put by one of the two possible responses. Notice
that the question on abstinence refers to those periods
when the husband was not away, not necessarily the total
periods between pregnancies.]

153

29. a. During the times when the woman was not pregnant, and during which her husband was not away, were there any times when she and her husband did not have intercourse for more than three months, for any reason?

    ____ yes (ask questions b, c, and d)

    ____ no (proceed to question 30)

						since last pregnancy
b. Before what pregnancies did these periods fall? (probe) (identification numbers)						
c. About how many months did each period of abstinence last? (number of months						
d. "For what reason did you avoid intercourse during these months? Was it to delay making you pregnant, or was it for some other reason?" (check one) to delay pregnancy						
some other reason						

30. "Some Lebanese couples think they know of ways to delay pregnancies. Have you ever heard of any method which some women use?"

    ____ yes

    ____ no (proceed to question 39)

154

31. "Will you tell me all of the methods you have heard about?
    (probe with "Have you heard of any other method?")
    (check each method mentioned)

    ____ safe period   ____ sponge

    ____ withdrawal   ____ diaphragm

    ____ sterilization   ____ jelly

    ____ late weaning   ____ other (describe) _____

    ____ condom   _____

    ____ douche   _____

       [Questions 30 and 31 are very sensitive questions.
You must ask them verbatim, but probe to make sure of
frank responses. Question 31 in particular calls for repeated probes to make sure that the woman is telling you
about all of the methods she has heard about; do not hint
at methods to help her. If she gives some method not listed,
be sure to describe that method under "other", no matter
whether or not you think the method actually does delay
pregnancies. Notice that late weaning is considered a
method in this question.]

32. "Have you and your husband ever attempted to delay any
    of your pregnancies by using any of the methods you
    have mentioned?"

    ____ yes

    ____ no (proceed to question 41)

		Next
33. Which pregnancies did the woman attempt to delay? (identification numbers)		
34. What methods did she use to delay this pregnancy? (list code numbers from list below)		
35. "For what reason did you and your husband want to delay this pregnancy?" (probe) (List code number of each reason mentioned.)		
36. "Which of these reasons was most important to you and your husband?" (write code number)		
37. Did the woman become pregnant while still attempting to avoid pregnancy? (check) yes (question 38) no (next pregnancy)		
38. What method was she using when she became pregnant? (code no.)		

(proceed to question 43)

Methods
1. Safe period
2. Withdrawal
3. Sterilization
4. Late weaning
5. Condom
6. Douche
7. Sponge
8. Diaphragm
9. Jelly
10. Other

Reasons for Attempting to Delay
1. Give rest to woman between pregnancies.
2. Give more personal attention to each child.
3. Financial limitations.
4. Children disliked or considered bothersome.
5. Wife wanted freedom for other activities.
6. Housing accommodations inadequate.
7. Husband's ill health, other than fatigue.
8. Wife's ill health, other than fatigue.
9. Wife's dislike of pregnancy and delivery.
10. Other or Don't know.

[Question 33. Again, you may have to refer to the pregnancy history questions in order to make sure that you get the correct pregnancy identification numbers. Ask all of the following questions for each pregnancy before going on to the next pregnancy.

Question 34. Identify the method or methods used to delay that pregnancy from the number or numbers in the list of methods below the table. If the woman says that she used more than one method, put the code number of each method used in a separate row in the column for that pregnancy. Probe for all methods.

Question 35. Do not give the woman a choice of alternatives, but let her express her reasons in her own words. For each reason given, put the code number of that reason in one of the rows. Then probe for any additional reasons, treating those reasons in the same way.

Question 36. Repeat the reasons that the woman has mentioned to you back to her. Then ask her which of these reasons was most important to her and her husband. Put the single code number of the most important reason in the indicated space.

Question 37. The point is to find whether the method the woman was using to delay pregnancy was effective or ineffective. If she became pregnant while using the method (even if through careless use of the method), then the method was ineffective, and "yes" should be checked. If, on the other hand, she was not using any method at the time she became pregnant, then the method was effective and "no" should be checked.

Question 38. This is to determine which method the woman was using that was ineffective for her on this pregnancy. She may have said that she used only one method before this pregnancy, in which case the number of that method can be inserted by the interviewer without asking. However, if she used more than one method previous to this pregnancy, you will have to ask which one she was using at the time she became pregnant.

Note: The "next pregnancy" column should contain all attempts to delay the pregnancy which has not yet occurred; that is, all methods used since the end of her last pregnancy.]

157

39. "If you and your husband had known of any method for delaying your pregnancies, do you believe that you ever would have attempted to delay any of your pregnances?"

_____ yes

_____ no (proceed to question 42)

40. a. "For what reasons would you and your husband have wanted to delay any of your pregnancies?"

(Probe by asking, "were there any reasons?")
(Put numbers of all reasons mentioned.)

(code number)

_____

_____

_____

_____

b. "Which of these reasons would have been the most important to you and your husband?"

_____ (proceed to question 43)

Reasons for Wanting to Delay Pregnancy

1. Give rest to the woman between pregnancies.
2. Give more personal attention to each child.
3. Financial limitations.
4. Children disliked or considered bothersome.
5. Wife wanted freedom for other activities.
6. Housing accommodations inadequate.
7. Husband's ill health, other than fatigue.
8. Wife's ill health, other than fatigue
9. Wife's dislike of pregnancy and delivery.
10. Other or Don't know.

41. a. "You say that you have heard of some method for de-
         laying pregnancy, but that you and your husband have
         never used any method. What reasons stopped you
         from using any method"?

                                              code numbers
         (Probe by asking "Were there any   _____
           other reasons?")
                                              _____
                                              _____
                                              _____

     b. "Which of these reasons was most important to you
         and your husband?"

         _____ (proceed to question 43)

42. a. "You say that you and your husband would not have used
         any method to delay any of your pregnancies, even if
         you had known of some method. What reasons would
         have stopped you from attempting to delay your
         pregnancies?"
                                              code numbers
         (Probe by asking "Were there any   _____
           other reasons?")
                                              _____
                                              _____
                                              _____

     b. "Which of these reasons was most important to you
         and your husband?"

         _____ (proceed to question 43)

Reasons for Not Attempting to Delay Pregnancies
1. Desire to have an unlimited number of children.
2. Desired number of children has not yet been reached.
3. Have enough daughters, but want more sons.
4. God ordains everything, including the number of
   children.
5. Religion forbids birth control.
6. Woman afraid of injuring her health.
7. Woman desires to keep her husband to herself by
   having children.
8. Contraceptive methods cost too much.
9. Husband forbids, without giving reasons.
10. Methods difficult or troublesome to use.
11. Neighbors would gossip.
12. Other.

159

"We have talked about your family and almost everything that might help doctors to explain the size of your family. I have only two more questions that I must ask on the subject.

"Doctors know that married couples are quite different in how often they choose to have intercourse. Doctors believe that this might help to explain the size of families these couples have. It would help these doctors to have this information about your family. I hope that you will answer these questions very frankly."

---

43. Ask about the first year the woman was married and living with her husband.

    "About how many times per month did you and your husband have intercourse?" (check one)

_____ 0 to 5 times	_____ 26 to 30 times	
_____ 6 to 10 times	_____ 31 to 35 times	
_____ 11 to 15 times	_____ 36 to 40 times	
_____ 16 to 20 times	_____ more than 40 times	
_____ 21 to 25 times	_____ don't know or refusal	

    (proceed to question 45)

44. (Ask this question only of woman who have had at least one live birth during the first five years of their marriages.)

    Ask about the period after the woman had recovered from her first live birth and before she became pregnant the next time.

    "About how many times per month did you and your husband have intercourse?" (check one)

_____ 0 to 5 times	_____ 26 to 30 times	
_____ 6 to 10 times	_____ 31 to 35 times	
_____ 11 to 15 times	_____ 36 to 40 times	
_____ 16 to 20 times	_____ more than 40 times	
_____ 21 to 25 times	_____ don't know or refusal	

160

45. a. "Suppose you had a very close friend, in the same cir-
       cumstances as yourself, and she asked you for advice
       on the convenient number of children for her. What
       is the number of children you would advise her to
       have, if she could?"   (probe and check)

       ____ woman would not give specific number (end the
                                               interview)

       ____ woman gave number, which was ____ (ask question b)

    b. "How many of these children should be boys, and how
       many girls?"

                              Number of boys ____

                              Number of girls ____

46. a. "Do you think your husband would agree with your advice
       to this woman?"

       ____ yes (end the interview)

       ____ no (ask question b)

       ____ don't know (end the interview)

    b. "How do you think his advice would be different from
       yours?" (check as many as necessary) (probe)

       ____ husband would advise more boys

       ____ husband would advise more girls

       ____ husband would advise fewer boys

       ____ husband would advise fewer girls

       ____ husband would not have an opinion on the
            ideal number

       ____ don't know exactly what husband would advise

       ____ other _____

                 _____

                 _____

[Answer the following questions after leaving the woman.]

47. Enumerator: _____
                    (family name)   (given name)

48. a. Date of interview: _____
                              (day)   (month)   (year)

     b. Time of interview: _____ to _____
                           (beginning)   (end)

49. Conditions of interview, if less than ideal (describe)

     _____

     _____

     _____

     _____

     _____

     _____

50. Residence of the woman.

     a. Village or section of Beirut (name) _____

     b. All information necessary to locate woman for reinter-
        view: (Use a map on the back of this page, if necessary.)

4. Index to the Interview Schedule

163

e. <u>Control Variables</u>

    Schedule identification number
    Present marital status of woman   1a
    Duration of marriage   1a, 1b, 6, 48a
    Year of marriage   6
    Consistency check; number of children living   23, 5b
    Consistency check; duration of marriage   5c, 6, 18a, 18b
                                         23, 48a

    Interviewer number
    Place of interview   50
    Composition of family   22, 23, 24

A P P E N D I X F

SUPPORTING TABLES

TABLE F-1

COMPUTATION OF TOTAL FERTILITY RATES
FOR ALL WOMEN IN YOUNGER GENERATION

Period of marriage		Women completing period married	Live births to these women during the period	Mean liv births p woman
In years (1)	In months (2)	(3)	(4)	(5)
0 to 5	0 thru 59	693	1,393	2.01
5 to 10	60 thru 119	494	824	1.67
10 to 15	120 thru 179	330	385	1.17
15 to 20	180 thru 239	196	168	0.86
20 to 25	240 thru 299	85	23	0.27
			Total of means or total fertility rate	5.98

TABLE F-2

MEAN LIVE BIRTHS PER WOMAN
IN THE TOTAL OLDER GENERATION
BY YEAR OF MARRIAGE

Year of marriage	Number of women	Mean live births per woman
1890 to 1909	13	6.6
1910 to 1919	38	6.6
1920 to 1928	88	6.8
Total	139	

TABLE F-3

MEAN LIVE BIRTHS PER WOMAN IN TOTAL YOUNGER GENERATION BY PERIOD OF MARRIAGE AND YEAR OF MARRIAGE

Year of marriage	Period of marriage (months since marriage)				
	0 to 59	60 to 119	120 to 179	180 to 239	240 to 300
1929 to 1933	2.10	1.62	1.15	0.75	0.26
1934 to 1938	1.80	1.72	1.20	0.94	
1939 to 1943	2.07	1.91	1.22		
1944 to 1948	2.06	1.71			
1949 to 1954	2.04				

TABLE F-4

TOTAL FERTILITY BY RESIDENCES OF COUPLES BEFORE AND AFTER MARRIAGE AND RELIGION OF HUSBAND

Residence of partners during five years before marriage	Residence of couple during five years after marriage	Older generation		Younger generation	
		Number of women	Mean live births per woman	Number of women	Total fertility rate
Moslem					
Both town or village	Town or village	29	7.31	173-12	7.42
Either city	Town or village	5	8.60	19-2	8.58
Either town or village	City	5	6.60	28-2	6.05
Both city	City	33	7.27	165-17	6.57
Christian					
Both town or village	Town or village	26	7.04	79-16	7.85
Either city	Town or village	5	5.20	16-3	3.86
Either town or village	City	10	5.20	53-7	3.76
Both city	City	22	4.45	156-26	3.66
Total		137		689*	

*Three women did not know the type of residence of the husband before marriage.

TOTAL FERTILITY BY RESIDENCES OF COUPLE AFTER MARRIAGE,
PLACE OF INTERVIEW, AND RELIGION OF HUSBAND

Residence after marriage	Place of interview	Older generation		Younger generation	
		Number of women	Mean live births per woman	Number of women	Total fertility rate
Moslem					
Town or village	Town or village	24	7.21	169-11	7.72
Town or village	City	11	8.09	14-2	7.61
City	City	38	7.21	201-19	6.61
Christian					
Town or village	Town or village	14	7.29	70-13	8.30
Town or village	City	18	6.33	26-6	4.54
City	City	32	4.69	211-33	3.70
Total		137		691*	

*One couple who were urban to rural migrants not included in table.

170

MEAN LIVE BIRTHS PER WOMAN IN OLDER GENERATION RESIDENT
IN TOWN OR VILLAGE AFTER MARRIAGE,
BY SOCIO ECONOMIC STATUS AND RELIGION OF HUSBAND

	Moslem		Christian	
Socio economic status	Number of women	Mean live births per woman	Number of women	Mean live births per woman
Education of couple				
Both illiterate	21	7.10	11	6.91
Either literate	14	8.07	21	6.67
Rooms per capita after marriage				
0.6 or less	21	7.19	15	6.80
0.7 or more	14	7.93	17	6.71
Occupation of husband after marriage*				
Farmer	19	7.53	18	7.33
Nonfarmer	13	7.62	13	6.15

*Eliminated three Moslems and one Christian whose husbands were non-self-supporting immediately after marriage.

TABLE F-7

MEAN LIVE BIRTHS PER WOMAN IN OLDER GENERATION INTERVIEWED
IN VILLAGE, BY SOCIO ECONOMIC STATUS AND
RELIGION OF HUSBAND

Socio economic status	Moslem		Christian	
	Number of women	Mean live births per woman	Number of women	Mean live birth per woman
Education of couple				
Both illiterate	18	6.94	10	6.80
Either literate	6	8.00	4	8.50
Rooms per capita after marriage				
0.6 or less	17	7.24	11	7.55
0.7 or more	7	7.14	3	6.33
Occupation of husband after marriage				
Farmer	18	7.50	13	7.31
Nonfarmer	6	6.33	1	7.00

TABLE F-8

YEARS OF SCHOOLING INVOLVED IN EDUCATION CLASSIFICATIONS

ebanese survey class	Minimum years of formal schooling	Most comparable Egyptian survey class
lliterate	0	Illiterate
iterate	0-5	Elementary**
lementary Certificate*	5	Primary**
ebanese Brivet*	9	Secondary**
ome degree higher than Brivet*	11 plus	University**

Refers to actual receipt of degree.

* Refers to level of education reached, but not completed. Based on Rizk, op. cit., Appendix C, Table 15, p. 182, and p. 21.

173

TABLE F-9

MEAN LIVE BIRTHS PER WOMAN IN OLDER GENERATION RESIDENT
IN CITY AFTER MARRIAGE, BY SOCIO ECONOMIC STATUS
AND RELIGION OF HUSBAND

Socio economic status	Moslem		Christian	
	Number of women	Mean live births per woman	Number of women	Mean live birth per woman
Elementary education certificate				
Neither possesses	32	7.19	24	4.00
Either possesses	6	7.33	8	6.75
Rooms per capita after marriage				
Less than one	11	6.36	9	5.33
One to two	22	7.73	12	4.83
Two or more	5	6.80	11	4.00

TABLE F-10

TOTAL FERTILITY RATES FOR YOUNGER GENERATION BY RESIDENCE
AFTER MARRIAGE, EDUCATION, AND RELIGION OF HUSBAND

Education of couple and residence after marriage	Moslem		Christian	
	Number of women	Total fertility rate	Number of women	Total fertility rate
Both illiterate				
Town or village	103-6	7.64	29-6	8.61
City	31-4	7.35	8-3	4.21
Difference		0.29		4.40
Either literate, but no elementary certificate				
Town or village	69-7	7.59	51-9	7.05
City	85-4	6.97	72-14	3.96
Difference		0.62		3.09
Either with elementary certificate				
Town or village	11-0	-	16-4	5.42
City	86-10	5.85	131-16	3.47
Difference		-		1.95
Total				
Town or village	183-13	7.65	96-19	7.18
City	202-20	6.53	211-33	3.70
Difference		1.12		3.48

TOTAL FERTILITY RATES FOR YOUNGER GENERATION BY RESIDENCE
AFTER MARRIAGE, ROOMS PER CAPITA AFTER MARRIAGE
AND RELIGION OF HUSBAND

Rooms per capita and residence after marriage	Moslem		Christian	
	Number of women	Total fertility rate	Number of women	Total fertility rate
Less than one room				
Town or village	156-13	7.80	60-13	7.21
City	57-7	7.08	28-4	4.51
Difference		0.72		2.70
One to two rooms				
Town or village	21-0	-	28-5	7.75
City	89-9	6.83	95-18	3.65
Difference		-		4.10
Two or more rooms				
Town or village	6-0	-	8-1	4.78
City	56-4	5.44	88-11	3.43
Difference		-		1.35
Total				
Town or village	183-13	7.65	96-19	7.18
City	202-20	6.53	211-33	3.70
Difference		1.12		3.48

TABLE F-12

MEAN LIVE BIRTHS PER WOMAN IN OLDER GENERATION BY RESIDENCE
AFTER MARRIAGE, EDUCATION, AND RELIGION OF HUSBAND

Education of couple and residence after marriage	Moslem		Christian	
	Number of women	Mean live births per woman	Number of women	Mean live births per woman
Both illiterate				
Town or village	21	7.10	11	6.91
City	10	6.80	4	2.75
Difference		0.30		4.16
Either literate, but no elementary certificate				
Town or village	11	8.64	20	6.65
City	22	7.36	20	4.25
Difference		1.28		2.40
Either with elementary certificate				
Town or village	3	6.00	1	7.00
City	6	7.33	8	6.75
Difference		-1.33		0.25
Total				
Town or village	35	7.49	32	6.75
City	38	7.21	32	4.69
Difference		0.28		2.06

TABLE F-13

MEAN LIVE BIRTHS PER WOMAN IN OLDER GENERATION BY RESIDENCE
AFTER MARRIAGE, ROOMS PER CAPITA AFTER MARRIAGE
AND RELIGION OF HUSBAND

Rooms per capita and residence after marriage	Moslem		Christian	
	Number of women	Mean live births per woman	Number of women	Mean live births per woman
Less than one room				
Town or village	24	7.58	18	7.17
City	11	6.36	9	5.33
Difference		1.22		1.84
One to two rooms				
Town or village	7	7.00	9	5.67
City	22	7.73	12	4.83
Difference		-0.73		0.84
More than two rooms				
Town or village	4	7.75	5	7.20
City	5	6.80	11	4.00
Difference		0.95		3.20
Total				
Town or village	35	7.49	32	6.75
City	38	7.21	32	4.69
Difference		0.28		2.06

TABLE F-14

TOTAL FERTILITY RATES FOR YOUNGER GENERATION RESIDENT IN CITY AFTER MARRIAGE
BY RELIGION OF HUSBAND AND EDUCATION OF COUPLE

	Elementary education certificate					
	Neither member possesses		Either member possesses		Total	
Religion	Number of women	Total fertility rate	Number of women	Total fertility rate	Number of women	Total fertility rate
Moslem	116-10	7.05	86-10	5.85	202-20	6.53
Christian	80-17	3.96	131-16	3.47	211-33	3.70
Difference		3.09		2.38		2.83

TABLE F-15

TOTAL FERTILITY RATES FOR YOUNGER GENERATION RESIDENT IN CITY AFTER MARRIAGE
BY RELIGION OF HUSBAND AND ROOMS PER CAPITA AFTER MARRIAGE

	Rooms per capita after marriage							
	Less than one		One to two		Two or more		Total	
Religion	Number of women	Total fertility rate	Number of women	Total fertility rate	Number of women	Total fertility rate	Number of women	Total fertility rate
Moslem	57-7	7.08	89-9	6.83	56-4	5.44	202-20	6.53
Christian	28-4	4.51	95-18	3.65	88-11	3.43	211-33	3.70
Difference		2.57		3.18		2.01		2.83

TABLE F-16

MEAN LIVE BIRTHS PER WOMAN IN OLDER GENERATION RESIDENT IN CITY AFTER MARRIAGE
BY RELIGION OF HUSBAND AND EDUCATION OF COUPLE

| | Elementary education certificate | | | | | |
| Religion | Neither member possesses | | Either member possesses | | Total | |
	Number of women	Mean live births per woman	Number of women	Mean live births per woman	Number of women	Mean live births per woman
Moslem	32	7.19	6	7.33	38	7.21
Christian	24	4.00	8	6.75	32	4.69
Difference		3.19		0.58		2.52

TABLE F-17

MEAN LIVE BIRTHS PER WOMAN IN OLDER GENERATION RESIDENT IN CITY AFTER MARRIAGE
BY RELIGION OF HUSBAND AND ROOMS PER CAPITA AFTER MARRIAGE

Religion	Rooms per capita after marriage							
	Less than one		One to two		Two or more		Total	
	Number of women	Mean live births per woman	Number of women	Mean live births per woman	Number of women	Mean live births per woman	Number of women	Mean live births per woman
Moslem	11	6.36	22	7.73	5	6.80	38	7.21
Christian	9	5.33	12	4.83	11	4.00	32	4.69
Difference		1.03		2.90		2.80		2.52

TABLE F-18

PERIOD—OF—MARRIAGE SPECIFIC FERTILITY RATES OF
SOCIAL BACKGROUND TYPES

Social background type	Mean live births per woman by five-year period*					Total fertility rate
	1st	2nd	3rd	4th	5th	
Village, uneducated						
1. Moslem	1.86	1.89	1.77	1.34	0.57	7.43
2. Christian	2.18	2.02	1.79	1.54	0.63	8.16
City, uneducated						
3. Moslem	2.29	2.05	1.44	1.07	0.50	7.35
4. Christian	1.90	1.19	0.67	0.29	0.09	4.14
City, educated						
5. Moslem	2.00	1.37	1.04	0.55	0.60	5.56
6. Christian	1.72	1.13	0.39	0.20	0.00	3.44

* Period-of-marriage specific rates also were computed for the sixth
five-year period of marriage. Only social-background types 1 and 3
had had any live births during the period; their specific rates were
low, 0.19 and 0.21 respectively. The sixth period of marriage was
not included in the computation of any total fertility rates.

TABLE F-19

PERCENTAGE DISTRIBUTIONS OF SOCIAL BACKGROUND TYPES
AMONG RELIGIOUS SECTS

Religious sect of husband	Village		City			
	Uneducated		Uneducated		Educated	
	Mos. (1)	Chr. (2)	Mos. (3)	Chr. (4)	Mos. (5)	Chr. (6)
	%	%	%	%	%	%
Sunni Moslem	33	-	74	-	84	-
Shiite Moslem	67	-	21	-	6	-
Druze	-	-	5	-	10	-
Maronite Catholic	-	100	-	43	-	27
Other Catholic	-	-	-	13	-	33
Greek Orthodox	-	-	-	43	-	34
Other Orthodox	-	-	-	1	-	3
Protestant	-	-	-	-	-	3
TOTAL	100%	100%	100%	100%	100%	100%
Number of women	184	76	136	96	49	107

TABLE F-20

PERCENTAGE DISTRIBUTIONS OF SOCIAL BACKGROUND TYPES
BY EDUCATION OF COUPLE

Highest education of couple	Village		City			
	Uneducated		Uneducated		Educated	
	Mos. (1)	Chr. (2)	Mos. (3)	Chr. (4)	Mos. (5)	Chr. (6)
	%	%	%	%	%	%
Neither literate	64	43	26	11	-	-
Either literate but no degree	36	57	74	89	-	-
Either with elementary certificate	-	-	-	-	-	-
Either with Lebanese Brivet	-	-	-	-	22	20
Either with some degree higher than Brivet	-	-	-	-	78	80
TOTAL	100%	100%	100%	100%	100%	100%
Number of women	184	76	136	96	49	107

TABLE F-21

PERCENTAGE DISTRIBUTIONS OF SOCIAL BACKGROUND TYPES
BY ROOMS PER CAPITA AFTER MARRIAGE

| Rooms per capita after marriage | Village | | City | | | |
| | Uneducated | | Uneducated | | Educated | |
	Mos. (1)	Chr. (2)	Mos. (3)	Chr. (4)	Mos. (5)	Chr. (6)
	%	%	%	%	%	%
Less than 1	90	72	38	30	12	1
1 to 2	9	25	43	44	49	44
2 to 3	1	3	15	21	27	33
3 or more	-	-	4	5	12	22
TOTAL	100%	100%	100%	100%	100%	100%
Number of women	184	76	136	96	49	107

TABLE F-22

PERCENTAGE DISTRIBUTIONS OF SOCIAL BACKGROUND TYPES
BY DECADE OF MARRIAGE

| | Village | | City | | | |
| | Uneducated | | Uneducated | | Educated | |
Decade of marriage	Mos. (1)	Chr. (2)	Mos. (3)	Chr. (4)	Mos. (5)	Chr. (6)
	%	%	%	%	%	%
1920-29	11	14	18	24	10	7
1930-39	32	26	21	32	16	21
1940-49	39	39	35	28	49	40
1950-54	18	20	25	16	24	32
TOTAL	100%	99%	99%	100%	99%	100%
Number of women	184	76	136	96	49	107

TABLE F-23

TOTAL FERTILITY RATES BY AGE OF WOMAN AT MARRIAGE
FOR WOMEN OF UNCONROLLED FERTILITY IN
UNEDUCATED VILLAGE MOSLEM SOCIAL BACKGROUND TYPE

| Age of woman at marriage | | | Total fertility | |
Class limits	Number of women	Mean age	Number of women	Rate
11 thru 13	22	12.5	22-3	7.72
14 thru 17	86	15.4	86-10	8.30
18 thru 22	56	19.6	56-11	5.96
TOTAL	164*		164*	

*
The total social background type numbered 184 wom-
en. Ten of these women were eliminated because
they had ever used conception control, induced
abortion, or been separated from their husbands for
more than three consecutive non-pregnant months.
Another ten women were married at ages older than
22; their number was not large enough to furnish
a stable total fertility rate.

TABLE F-24

MEAN MONTHS BETWEEN MARRIAGE AND FIRST LIVE BIRTH
BY AGE OF WOMAN AT MARRIAGE

Age of woman at marriage	Number of women	Mean months
11 to 13	30	25.5
14 to 17	299	16.6
18 to 22	267	15.6
23 to 27	87	16.6
TOTAL	683*	

* Included all women married in or after 1920, except (1) women who did not have a live birth
during the first 60 months of marriage, (2) women
who had attempted to delay any conception before
the first live birth in any way, (3) women who
had been separated from their husbands for more
than three consecutive non-pregnant months before
the first live birth, (4) women who had induced
an abortion before the first live birth, (5) three
women who did not know their ages at marriage,
and (6) twenty-nine otherwise qualified women
married at ages of 28 or more.

TABLE F-25

AGE OF WOMAN AT MARRIAGE BY SOCIAL BACKGROUND TYPE

Social background type	Years of age at marriage							Number of women*	Mean
	11-13	14-17	18-22	23-27	28-32	33+	Total		
Village, uneducated									
1. Moslem	12%	49%	32%	6%	1%	0%	100%	183	17.2
2. Christian	3	58	25	12	1	1	100	76	18.1
City, uneducated									
3. Moslem	2	53	36	7	2	0	100	135	17.9
4. Christian	0	22	49	18	7	4	100	96	21.2
City, educated									
5. Moslem	0	39	45	14	2	0	100	49	19.0
6. Christian	0	23	41	29	6	1	100	106	21.1

* N equals 645. Eliminated three women who did not know ages at marriage.

TABLE F-26

PER CENT OF NON-PREGNANT MONTHS SPENT IN PROLONGED SEPARATIONS
FROM HUSBAND BY SOCIAL BACKGROUND TYPE

ocial background type	Number of women	Per cent of non-pregnant months separated
llage, uneducated		
1. Moslem	156	0.2%
2. Christian	58	0.2
ty, uneducated		
3. Moslem	106	0.8
4. Christian	62	1.9
ty, educated		
5. Moslem	44	1.3
6. Christian	91	1.2
TOTAL	517*	

Does not include 131 women married more than twenty five years.

TABLE F-27

PER CENT OF CITY WOMEN MARRIED MORE THAN TEN YEARS EVER USING
CONCEPTION CONTROL METHODS, BY EDUCATION AND RELIGION

Method	Uneducated			Educated		
	Mos. 3	Cath. 4a	Orth. 4b	Mos. 5	Cath. 6a	Orth 6b
	%	%	%	%	%	%
Any non-appliance method	44	54	47	51	47	65
abstinence to delay	1	0	0	0	0	0
withdrawal	43	54	47	49	40	50
safe period	3	0	5	9	9	23
Any appliance method	34	29	24	60	49	50
condom	21	24	16	54	33	46
douch (irrigation)	8	5	8	9	7	8
sponge (or cotton tampon, impregnated)	7	5	3	9	2	0
diaphragm (or pessary)	2	0	3	6	12	0
jelly (or suppository)	6	2	0	9	2	0
Other temporary method	11	2	11	3	5	8
Sterilization	1	2	0	0	9	12
Any method	60	59	53	83	81	92
Number of women	98	41	38	35	43	26

* Includes three Protestants.

TABLE F-28

MEDIAN DAUGHTERS AND MEDIAN SONS ADVISED BY WOMEN
BY SOCIAL BACKGROUND TYPE

Social background type	Number of women	Median daughters advised	Median sons advised	Sex ratio of medians
Village, uneducated				
1. Moslem	46	2.0	3.0	1.5
2. Christian	33	1.7	2.4	1.4
City, uneducated				
3. Moslem	98	1.7	2.2	1.3
4. Christian	60	1.8	2.3	1.3
City, educated				
5. Moslem	43	1.8	2.0	1.1
6. Christian	94	1.8	2.1	1.2
TOTAL	374*			

*Includes only women who were willing to give specific numbers for both sons and daughters.

YEAR OF MARRIAGE BY RESIDENCE IMMEDIATELY AFTER MARRIAGE,
EDUCATION OF COUPLE, AND RELIGION OF HUSBAND

Residence of couple during
first five years after marriage

Highest education of either member	Year of marriage				Number of women
Religion of husband	Before 1920	1920 to 1939	1940 to 1954	Total	
City					
Illiterate					
Moslem	14.3%	31.0%	54.7%	100.0%	42
Christian	8.3	58.3	33.3	99.9	12
Literate					
Moslem	8.8	36.8	54.4	100.0	114
Christian	13.0	48.0	39.0	100.0	100
Elementary Certificate					
Moslem	2.3	38.6	59.1	100.0	44
Christian	6.2	34.4	59.4	100.0	32
Brivet or higher					
Moslem	0.0	25.5	74.5	100.0	51
Christian	1.8	27.5	70.6	99.9	109
Town or Village					
Illiterate					
Moslem	9.0	45.1	45.8	99.9	133
Christian	24.4	33.3	42.2	99.9	45
Literate					
Moslem	6.1	34.2	59.8	100.1	82
Christian	13.2	46.1	40.8	100.1	76
Elementary Certificate or higher					
Moslem	7.1	21.4	71.4	99.9	14
Christian	10.5	47.4	42.1	100.0	19
TOTAL					873

TABLE F-30

EDUCATION OF THE WOMAN BY HIGHEST EDUCATION OF THE COUPLE, RESIDENCE AFTER MARRIAGE, AND RELIGION OF THE HUSBAND

Residence immediately after marriage

Highest education attained by either member

Religion of the husband	Education of the Woman					Number of women*
	Illiterate	Literate	Elementary Certificate	Lebanese Brivet or Higher	Total	
City						
Literate						
Moslem	42.1%	57.9%			100.0%	114
Christian	25.0%	75.0%			100.0%	100
Elementary Certificate						
Moslem	29.5%	20.4%	50.0%		99.9%	44
Christian	25.0%	12.5%	62.5%		100.0%	32
Brivet or Higher						
Moslem	7.8%	17.6%	31.4%	43.1%	99.9%	51
Christian	3.7%	15.6%	17.4%	63.3%	100.0%	109
Town or Village						
Literate						
Moslem	92.7%	7.3%			100.0%	82
Christian	59.2%	40.8%			100.0%	76
Elementary Certificate						
Moslem	0.0%	75.0%	25.0%		100.0%	4
Christian	16.7%	16.7%	66.7%		100.1%	6
Brivet or Higher						
Moslem	30.0%	20.0%	40.0%	10.0%	100.0%	10
Christian	7.7%	23.1%	23.1%	46.2%	100.1%	13

* N = 641. Does not include couples with both members illiterate.

TABLE F-31

PAID WORK OF WOMAN DURING FIVE YEARS BEFORE MARRIAGE,
BY RESIDENCE AFTER MARRIAGE, EDUCATION OF COUPLE, AND
RELIGION OF HUSBAND

Residence after marriage Highest education of either member Religion of husband	Did not work for money	Best-paying position working mostly		Total	N
		At home	Away from home		
	(1)	(2)	(3)	(4)	
City					
Illiterate					
Moslem	83.3%	4.8%	11.9%	100.0%	42
Christian	33.3%	25.0%	41.7%	100.0%	12
Literate					
Moslem	86.6%	8.0%	5.4%	100.0%	112*
Christian	65.7%	12.1%	22.2%	100.0%	99*
Elementary Certificate					
Moslem	86.4%	9.1%	4.6%	100.1%	44
Christian	65.6%	6.2%	28.2%	100.0%	32
Brivet or higher					
Moslem	90.2%	2.0%	7.8%	100.0%	51
Christian	83.5%	2.7%	13.8%	100.0%	109
Town or Village					
Illiterate					
Moslem	91.7%	1.5%	6.9%	100.1%	132*
Christian	91.1%	4.4%	4.4%	99.9%	45
Literate					
Moslem	92.7%	1.2%	6.1%	100.0%	82
Christian	88.2%	2.6%	9.2%	100.0%	76
Elementary Certificate					
Moslem	100.0%	0.0%	0.0%	100.0%	4
Christian	100.0%	0.0%	0.0%	100.0%	6
Brivet or higher					
Moslem	90.0%	0.0%	10.0%	100.0%	10
Christian	76.9%	0.0%	23.1%	100.0%	13

* N = 869. Two women of no religious identification were eliminated. Four women answered "don't know" to questions on pre-marital occupation.

TABLE F-32

MEAN NUMBER OF WOMAN'S SIBLINGS LIVING AT TIME OF HER MARRIAGE,
BY RESIDENCE AFTER MARRIAGE, EDUCATION OF COUPLE, AND RELIGION OF HUSBAND

Highest education of either member	Residence after marriage			
	City		Town or village	
Religion of husband	Mean	N	Mean	N
Illiterate				
Moslem	4.4	42	4.4	133
Christian	4.8	12	5.7	45
Literate				
Moslem	4.7	114	4.5	82
Christian	4.4	100	5.1	76
Elementary Certificate				
Moslem	4.6	43*	5.2	4
Christian	4.6	32	4.8	6
Brivet or higher				
Moslem	4.6	51	4.4	10
Christian	3.9	109	4.5	13

* One case answered "don't know" to the question.
N = 872.

RESIDENCE HISTORIES OF COUPLES BY RESIDENCE IMMEDIATELY AFTER MARRIAGE,
EDUCATION OF COUPLE, AND RELIGION OF HUSBAND

Residence of couple during
five years after marriage

Highest education of either member	Per cent in City			
	During five years before marriage		At	
Religion of man	woman	man	interview	N

City
Illiterate

Moslem	88.1%	90.2%	100.0%	42
Christian	66.7	100.0	100.0	12

Literate

Moslem	85.1	94.7	99.1	114
Christian	72.0	82.8*	100.0	100

Elementary Certificate

Moslem	93.2	95.5	100.0	44
Christian	81.2	90.3*	100.0	32

Brivet or higher

Moslem	96.1	88.2	100.0	51
Christian	84.4	94.4*	100.0	109

Town or Village
Illiterate

Moslem	1.5%	2.3%	4.5%	133
Christian	2.2	2.2	11.1	45

Literate

Moslem	3.7	3.7*	13.4	82
Christian	7.9	10.7*	42.1	76

Elementary Certificate

Moslem	75.0	33.3*	100.0	4
Christian	50.0	33.3	66.7	6

Brivet or higher

Moslem	20.0	10.0	50.0	10
Christian	46.1	75.0*	100.0	13

N=873*

* Indicates one case of unknown information, not used in computations.

TABLE F-34

MEDIAN ROOMS PER CAPITA IMMEDIATELY AFTER MARRIAGE BY
RESIDENCE AFTER MARRIAGE, EDUCATION OF COUPLE,
AND RELIGION OF HUSBAND

Highest education of either member	Type of residence after marriage			
	City		Town or village	
Religion of husband	Median	N	Median	N
Illiterate				
Moslem	0.8	42	0.4	133
Christian	1.0	12	0.5	45
Literate				
Moslem	1.2	114	0.5	82
Christian	1.5	100	0.7	76
Elementary Certificate				
Moslem	1.5	44	1.4	4
Christian	1.8	32	0.7	6
Brivet or higher				
Moslem	1.8	51	1.6	10
Christian	2.1	109	1.6	13

N = 873.

TABLE F-35

MAIN OCCUPATION OF HUSBAND DURING FIRST FIVE YEARS AFTER MARRIAGE BY RESIDENCE OF COUPLE IMMEDIATELY AFTER MARRIAGE, EDUCATION OF COUPLE, AND RELIGION OF HUSBAND

Residence of couple after marriage / Highest education of either member / Religion of man	Main source of income								Total	N
	Nonfarming					Farming				
	Profession (1)	commerce or Industry (2)	clerical (3)	skilled work or craft (4)	unskilled work or servant (5)	owning some land (7)	owning no land (8)	Other than own work (6)		
City										
Illiterate										
Moslem	0.0%	16.7%	0.0%	14.3%	33.3%	2.4%	0.0%	33.3%	100.0%	42
Christian	0.0	16.7	0.0	16.7	50.0	8.3	0.0	8.3	100.0	12
Literate										
Moslem	2.6	28.9	6.1	15.8	39.5	0.9	0.0	6.1	99.9	114
Christian	4.0	26.0	6.0	44.0	19.0	0.0	0.0	1.0	100.0	100
Elementary Cert.										
Moslem	2.3	45.5	4.5	25.0	18.2	0.0	0.0	4.5	100.0	44
Christian	12.5	40.6	6.2	25.0	15.6	0.0	0.0	0.0	99.9	32
Brivet or higher										
Moslem	25.5	39.2	21.6	9.8	3.9	0.9	0.0	0.0	100.0	51
Christian	28.4	35.8	22.9	10.1	0.9	0.9	0.0	0.9	99.9	109
Town or village										
Illiterate										
Moslem	0.0%	7.6%	0.0%	0.0%	13.0%	33.6%	42.7%	3.1%	100.0	131*
Christian	0.0	2.2	0.0	4.4	13.3	60.0	17.8	2.2	99.9	45
Literate										
Moslem	0.0	11.0	2.4	1.2	14.6	48.8	19.5	2.4	99.9	82
Christian	1.3	17.1	0.0	11.8	9.2	55.3	2.6	2.6	99.9	76
Elementary Cert. or higher										
Moslem	28.6	21.4	7.1	21.4	14.3	0.0	7.1	0.0	99.9	14
Christian	36.8	26.3	5.3	5.3	15.8	10.5	0.0	0.0	100.0	19

* Eliminated two cases of husbands who were farmers, but whose wives did not know whether they owned land. N = 871.

TABLE F-36

PERCENTAGE DISTRIBUTION OF COITAL FREQUENCY BY SOCIAL BACKGROUND TYPE FOR TWO TIME PERIODS

Social background type	Per cent having coital frequency per month											
	During first year of marriage						Between first live birth and next pregnancy					
	0-11	11-20	21-30	31+	Total	N	0-10	11-20	21-30	31+	Total	N
Village, uneducated												
1. Moslem	11%	24%	42%	23%	100%	165	23%	33%	36%	8%	100%	164
2. Christian	23	37	26	14	100	70	45	36	17	1	99	69
City, uneducated												
3. Moslem	19	36	29	16	100	134	39	34	16	11	100	131
4. Christian	12	40	35	13	100	92	37	48	14	1	100	87
City, educated												
5. Moslem	10	38	25	27	100	48	30	36	19	15	100	47
6. Christian	15	47	23	15	100	106	37	41	13	9	100	104
N						615*						602**

* Does not include 33 women who refused to answer the question on frequency of intercourse, 19 of them from social background type 1.

** Does not include 11 women who refused to answer the question on frequency of intercourse, 6 of them from social background type 1. Also excludes women who had no live birth.

APPENDIX G

REFERENCES CITED

Back, Kurt W., and J. Mayone Stycos. The Survey under Unusual
Conditions: Methodological Facets of the Jamaica Human
Fertility Investigation. Cornell University, Ithaca, New
York: Society for Applied Anthropology, Monograph Number
1, 1959.

Chruchill, Charles W. The City of Beirut: A Socio-Economic
Survey. Beirut, Lebanon: Dar El-Kitab, 1954.

Coale, Ansley J., and Edgar M. Hoover. Population Growth and
Economic Development in Low-Income Countries: A Case Study
of India's Prospects. Princeton: Princeton University
Press, 1958.

Davis, Kingsley, and Judith Blake. "Social Structure and Fertility: An Analytical Framework," Economic Development and
Cultural Change, 4 (April, 1956), 211-235.

Guttmacher, A. F. "Fertility of Man," Fertility and Sterility,
III (May-June, 1952), 281-289.

Hatt, Paul K. Backgrounds of Human Fertility in Puerto Rico:
A Sociological Survey. Princeton: Princeton University
Press, 1952.

Hitti, Philip K. Lebanon in History. London: MacMillan and
Co., Ltd., 1957.

Hourani, A. H. Syria and Lebanon: A Political Essay. New York
Oxford University Press, 1946.

Human Relations Area Files, Inc. The Republic of Lebanon, Volume I. New Haven: Box 2054 Yale Station, 1956.

Henry, Louis. "Intervals between Confinements in the Absence of Birth Control," Eugenics Quarterly, 5 (December, 1958), 200-211.

Hill, Reuben, J. Mayone Stycos, and Kurt W. Back. The Family and Population Control: A Puerto Rican Experiment in Social Change. Chapel Hill: University of North Carolina Press, 1959.

Hyrenius, H. "Fertility and Reproduction in a Swedish Population Group without Family Limitation," Population Studies, XII (November, 1958), 121-130.

Lorimer, Frank, et al. Culture and Human Fertility. Paris: United Nations Educational, Scientific and Cultural Organization, 1954.

MacLeod, J., and R. Z Gold. "The Male Factor in Fertility and Infertility: Semen Quality and Certain Other Factors in Relation to Ease of Conception," Fertility and Sterility, 4 (January-February, 1953), 10-33.

Montagu, M. F. Ashley. The Reproductive Development of the Female. New York: The Julian Press, 1957.

Potter, Robert G., Jr. "Length of the Fertile Period," forthcoming in the Milbank Memorial Fund Quarterly.

Rizk, Hanna. "Fertility Patterns in Selected Areas in Egypt." Unpublished Ph. D. dissertation, Princeton University, June, 1959.

Ryder, Norman B. "Fertility," The Study of Population, Philip
    M. Hauser and Otis Dudley Duncan, editors. Chicago:
    University of Chicago Press, 1959. Chapter 18.

Sharman, A. "Ovulation after Pregnancy," Fertility and Steril-
    ity, II (September-October, 1951), 371-393.

Singh, Sohan, and John B. Wyon. "An Edidemiological Study of
    the Population Problem in North India," Fifth Inter-
    national Conference on Planned Parenthood: Report of the
    Proceedings, 24-29 October, 1955, Tokyo, Japan. London:
    International Planned Parenthood Federation, 1955, 75-80.

Stix, Regina K. "Birth Control in a Mid-Western City; I," Mil-
    bank Memorial Fund Quarterly, 17 (January, 1939), 69-91.

_____, "Factors Underlying Individual and Group Differences
    in Uncontrolled Fertility," Milbank Memorial Fund Quarterly
    xxviii (July, 1940), 239-256.

_____, and Frank W. Notestein. Controlled Fertility. Balti-
    more: Williams and Wilkins Co., 1940.

Stycos, J. Mayone. Family and Fertility in Puerto Rico: A Study
    of the Lower Income Group. New York: Columbia University
    Press, 1955.

United Nations, Department of Social Affairs, Population Divi-
    sion. Multilingual Demographic Dictionary, Provisory
    Edition. Population Studies, No. 19. New York: United
    Nations, 1954.

Westoff, Charles F., Robert G. Potter, Jr., Philip C. Sagi, and
    Elliot G. Mishler. Family Growth in Metropolitan America.
    Princeton: Princeton University Press, forthcoming.